NOT JUST UP AND DOWN

UNDERSTANDING MOOD IN BIPOLAR DISORDER

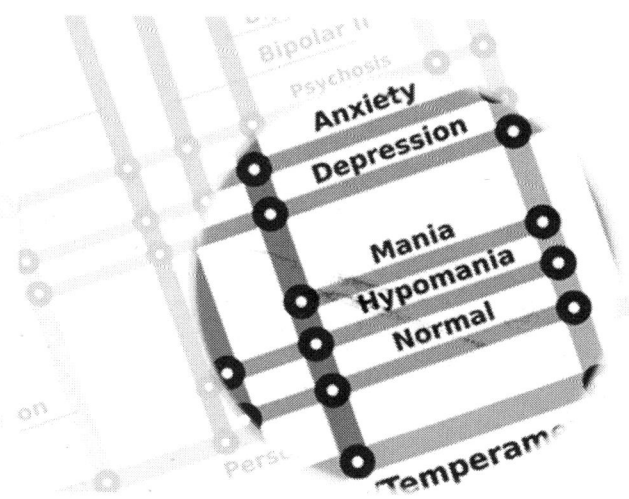

JOHN McMANAMY

The Bipolar Expert Series

mcman

www.bipolarexpertseries.com

ISBN 978-0-9852394-3-5

In Loving Memory

Kevin Greim: 1980-2008

CONTENTS

Part One: Mapping Bipolar ... 1

Chapter One
Getting to know us

Chapter Two
An introduction to cycles, starring Emil Kraepelin

Chapter Three
First, the Standard Version

Chapter Four
The DSM: Evolution of the Standard Version

Chapter Five
The DSM: How the most influential psychiatrist no one ever heard of rescued us from Freud

Chapter Six
The DSM: Busting the Myth

Chapter Seven
The DSM: Killing Buddha

Chapter Eight
Personality and Temperament

Chapter Nine
Is it normal or is it bipolar?

Chapter Ten
Bipolar - Here we are, this is what we put up with, but where the hell did it come from?

Chapter Eleven
The map to reality

Part Two: Mapping Mood ... 62

Chapter Twelve
The bipolar spectrum and recurrence

PART ONE: MAPPING BIPOLAR

"O, let me not be mad, not mad, sweet heaven! Keep me
in temper; I would not be mad!"

—Shakespeare, King Lear

1. GETTING TO KNOW US

My goal in this book is to help make you an expert patient. Here's the deal: Patients who take the lead in learning about their illness and in managing their own recovery fare far better than those who simply wait for something to happen. This applies across all chronic illnesses, not just bipolar disorder.

I can cite numerous studies. Let me instead share with you some of my personal story. Soon after I was diagnosed in early 1999, I began researching my illness, then writing about it. My plan was to learn as I went along. By writing about my illness, I would, over time, become my own expert.

Since I used to be a financial journalist, this was not an entirely daft idea. My first job out of law school back in the early eighties involved writing summaries of high court decisions for a legal publishing company. In nothing flat I became a master of distilling 50 pages of densely-worded gobbledygook into four or five crystal-clear sentences. Six or seven, tops.

I applied this same technique to my new email newsletter, *McMan's Depression and Bipolar Weekly*. This time, I turned scientific studies into plain English. I also provided short summaries of books and current events and other goings-on. "Knowledge is Necessity" became my tagline. My goal was to help make others—people like me—their own experts.

The response to my newsletter was overwhelmingly positive. A website, *McMan's Depression and Bipolar Web*, soon followed. Eventually I was able to eke out a living. I was putting in 70 and 80-hour weeks. As well as providing summaries, now I was starting to connect the dots into longer pieces. This meant corresponding with researchers, clinicians, and authors, advocates, plus patients and loved ones. I was also attending conferences.

It didn't stop there. Bipolar also consumed my social life. At one point, in New Jersey, I was facilitating two support groups a week.

Over time, I picked up a whole new set of critical-thinking and knowledge-related skills. These were exciting times. New scientific discoveries had the effect of turning everyone into novices, even the experts. We were all learning together.

When I started out as a financial journalist way back, I operated on the principle that it would take me five years to become truly skilled in my craft and another five to master it. I adopted the same attitude to writing about my illness, with this proviso: This time my skin was in the game, and I was dealing with an illness that takes no prisoners.

Bipolar is not an option. A manic episode during the late eighties snatched away my career. Suicidal depressions in the nineties drained me of my soul. My erratic behavior from both decades cut me off from humanity. My only option, at age 49, was to reach acceptance with my condition and learn to live with it. Those early newsletters literally saved my life.

Below is a quick copy and paste from one of my early efforts:

McMan's Depression and Bipolar Weekly
July 11, 2004 Vol 6 No 17

Welcome
Lead Story: Researchers are taking a new approach to hunting for

genetic and biological markers for mood, with enormous implications for diagnosis and treatment.

Also in this issue: Summer of the endophenotype (the thalamus, GABA, suicidal brains, REM sleep), Important reader notice, Neonatal complications and ADs, Abilify in Europe, TMAP, When meds turn on you, Attitudes changing, Kids warehoused, More cuts, More on AD suicide controversy, Are depression and BP part of the same spectrum?, Drug industry paranoia, Free meds, The law no one heard of, Depressed in action, A patient's eloquent testimony, McMan's Web, Donations.

Endo de Phenotype

Hussein Manji MD is no stranger to this Newsletter. In an article in this month's "Neuropsychopharmacology," Dr Manji and his co-authors at the NIMH elaborate on what they've been up to lately - something to do with "endophenotypes" in depression. ...

Five and a half years into it—in late 2004—I felt sufficiently confident to take on writing a book. I would tackle the scientific and clinical issues from a patient's perspective. To my knowledge, with regard to my illness, this was the first time this had been done. Patients are supposed to write memoirs and leave the expert stuff to experts. I did not hold out much hope of finding a publisher.

Against all odds, my manuscript landed on the desk of an enlightened editor, Sarah Durand, to whom I shall forever be grateful. Soon after, late in 2005 HarperCollins offered me a contract. In October 2006, my book, *Living Well with Depression and Bipolar Disorder,* came out.

Several months later, I received a surprise email. The International Conference on Bipolar Disorders was to honor me with a public service award at their conference in 2007. The researchers and clinicians who frequented these gatherings were the people who had dedicated their lives to improving mine. I had read their books and articles, attended their seminars, corresponded with them, interviewed them.

If I were capable of tears, I would have blubbered up a storm. Never underestimate the power of recognition. Finally, after all these years …

By this time, I was living in southern California, seeking out new personal and social outlets, carving out a new identity. I allotted myself more free time, and spent a good deal of it out in nature. A sense of balance entered my life. But for that to happen, I had to let go of my newsletter and cut down on attending conferences.

I stayed in the game by blogging and being involved in mental health advocacy. By this time, I was contemplating an existence that had nothing to do with bipolar, but a voice in my head told me I wasn't done. My friends were telling me the same thing. There was another book in me, begging to be written.

All these years later, I am surprised by how well my *Living Well* book has held up. If I were to update it, I would only change a few things. Nevertheless, were I to write it again, it would look completely different. So here we are—right here, right now—my first book in this series, the *Bipolar Expert Series*.

By bipolar expert, I am talking about you. In this first book, we will look at moods in depth. We have all been told pretty much the same story, but what if I were to tell you that story is at best half-true? In this book, we fill in the blanks, and in the process bust a few myths.

Later books in this series will explore behavior, treatment, recovery, science, and relationships. But before we can make any headway in those areas, first we need to know ourselves. It's not simply about having awareness of our depressions and manias and so on. It's also about finding our own true sense of "normal."

Typically, the expert author assumes a detached and disinterested perspective. To the expert, the brain is biological wiring, the disease takes this course or that course, and human beings are statistics and case studies. The takeaway: Listen to your doctor, find a therapist, take your meds, practice healthy lifestyle routines, be hopeful. Finished, done.

Living Well wasn't at all like that, but at the same time I didn't stray too far outside the lines. This book is different. On one hand, you will read a detailed scientific and clinical narrative, carefully researched and grounded in the findings of the leading experts. But that narrative runs side-by-side with my own ruminations.

Let me explain ...

Back when I wrote *Living Well*, I saw myself as a sort of middleman. I sought out expert information and processed it in a way that I thought might be useful to you. My own way of looking at things, of course, shaped the narrative, but I tried to stay out of the way as much as possible.

Where I did reveal my personal side, it was in the context of past depressions and manias. You didn't see my present self, and this may have created the wrong impression that I had somehow found my way back to normal, or within reasonable proximity.

This book has a totally different perspective. Fifteen years of near-total immersion in bipolar—some 50,000 accumulated work hours later—I have no hesitation in inserting myself into the narrative. This time, the expert information I present is seen through my own eyes, processed by my own experience.

I am trusting this approach humanizes our shared experiences, unites us in some mysterious way, and in the process we all assume ownership of our vast wisdom and experience. But for that to happen, I need to come out of hiding, step into broad daylight, reveal my present self. Hardly the model of someone who has it all together. Far from it. What you will see, instead, is a work in progress.

In dealing with bipolar, as with life, there is no such thing as a finished product. I'm trusting you can relate to that. Let's see what happens ...

2. AN INTRODUCTION TO CYCLES, STARRING EMIL KRAEPELIN

It's time …

When I step out of the house, I go through the same mental checklist as everyone else—keys, wallet, phone, on and on. But I'm also performing a systems check on my brain. This sort of thing runs in the background all the time, but when I'm headed out the door the exercise assumes the quality of anal-retentive high drama, like a shuttle launch countdown ...

Make sure my head is screwed on right.

Ha! If people only knew. I live with bipolar. Most of the time I go about my life as if I don't have it, but that is only because I take nothing—including an operational brain—for granted. Breathe! I remind myself. All systems go. I'm ready to face the music.

Bipolar is entirely the wrong term for my illness, your illness. "Cycling" is far more apt, suggesting the brain in perpetual motion—moods, thoughts, perceptions, everything—nothing standing still, everything shifting, nothing predictable.

But is there anything up ahead I can at least anticipate?

Day slips into night, the moon waxes and wanes—my brain is a veritable *I Ching*. I may head out into the world cool, calm, and collected, but will my brain be working for me two hours from now when it really matters? I already know what I'll be like on the way home, a wrung-out dish rag, too spent to stop off at Trader Joe's. Is there enough food in the fridge?

Breathe! I remind myself. Breathe.

Way back in 1851, the French psychiatrist Jean-Pierre

Falret came up with *la folie circulaire* (circular insanity) to explain the continuous pattern of depression, mania, and "normal" that he observed in his patients.

In 1899, the pioneering German diagnostician Emil Kraepelin coined the term "manic-depressive insanity" to describe what he saw as a much wider and more complex phenomenon. Nevertheless, cycling was the central piece to the puzzle. In 1915, he wrote: "The course of manic–depressive insanity is marked by a recurrence of attacks separated by lucid intervals."

In the 1921 English translation to his classic *Manic-Depressive Insanity and Psychosis*, Kraepelin describes the illness as including "the whole domain of so-called periodic and circular insanity."

Don't be frightened by the word, insanity. That's just how people talked in those days.

What we call bipolar is an enormously complex condition, but strip it to its most essential element and what we're left with can best be described as a "cycling illness." Simply knowing that we have ups and downs is not sufficient. What we need to know is how these ups and downs relate, what is driving them, and what else is interacting with the dynamic.

Our "episodes" (depressed, manic, hypomanic, anxiety, and "normal") only make sense in the context of the cycle that propels them. Is our hypomania (mania lite), for instance, nothing to worry about or is it a prelude to a crushing depression? Maybe it's signaling we are about to get swept up in a full tidal mania.

Oh crap! Here we go again.

No, I'll be fine. Depression is my real nemesis, extinction my constant temptation. Mania, by contrast, is more of a distant ancestral memory. As long as I'm rested, as long as I'm not overstimulated, as long as I can space out my day, I can count on my brain reasonably cooperating with me.

Look both ways before crossing. No running with scissors, no playing with matches. Stop, look, and listen.

It's easy, right? Except that Kraepelin, when writing about mood, gave us detailed accounts of how our energy levels—what he described as excitement and fatigue—impacted our thinking and motivation. Thinking and motivation, in turn, engaged in a sort of out-of-phase *danse macabre* with our moods, everything shifting and changing and turning—the whole *I Ching* thing—with the passing of time.

In other words, my depression—or, for that matter, my "normal"—is going to look a lot different with my thoughts running away from me and the power turned up to full than when someone suddenly pulls the plug or my thoughts wind down like a spent mainspring.

Do the math, calculate the endless variations.

Now let's throw in circadian rhythms—our sleep and wake cycles—plus every process that regulates homeostasis, all that mysterious biology that keeps our body and brain function relatively constant. And while we're at it, let's not overlook all those Stone Age artifacts, including those imperceptible glacial drifts that prepared our ancestors for the change in the seasons.

Kay Jamison, in her 1999 *Night Falls Fast*, describes it this way:

We are, with the rest of life, periodic creatures, beholden for our rhythms to the rotations of the earth around the sun and the moon around the earth. The chemistry of our brains and bodies oscillates in adaptation to the earth's fluctuations in heat and light, and probably its electromagnetic fields as well. Like other mammals, our patterns of eating, sleeping, and other physical activities sway with the seasons, varying in accordance with changes in day length and temperature. A master biological clock, genetically determined, controls the cycling of our brain's constituent chemicals and shapes our responses to our physical environment.

Just so we're clear: We are talking many cycles, not just one. Cycles within cycles, if you like. Throw any one of them out of whack and there goes your precision timing, your sense of being in control. Then life becomes a mad scramble, like juggling spinning plates.

Inevitably, it happens, a plate flies out of reach. Maybe you simply cut your loss and carry on. Or maybe comes the horrible realization that yet once more things have slipped away from you. Everything is about to come crashing down. And there you are, alone in the bitter awful aftermath, left to pick up the pieces.

My day hasn't gone too well. A series of email exchanges indicates I am headed into the meeting from hell. My brain wasn't built for this. Should I just text my apologies?

Other people make plans. We make life-or-death risk assessments. Often, our illness mandates that we play it safe, not tempt fate. But if we don't take risks, we lose out on all those life-affirming experiences that define us as human. Call it the bipolar's dilemma: Take a chance and we risk losing control of our brains. Play it safe and we isolate ourselves from humanity.

When all is said and done, there are no right or wrong decisions, only informed and uninformed ones. Breathe! All systems go.

I pull into the parking lot. Suddenly, every one of the billion neurons beneath my skull is screaming at me to put the car into reverse and lay down a strip of rubber getting the hell out. Instead, I turn off the ignition and collect myself.

I'm seated at the table. The inspiration for the character Cruela De Vil walks in, ignores me, and gives her devoted henchman an exaggerated hug. Everything normal. An hour later, things go horribly wrong. Ms De Vil outdoes herself. Against stupidity, even the gods battle in vain. I never saw it coming.

Back in the car, my brain is Three-Mile Island. I am in partial melt-down, past the point of no-return. None of my many coping tricks will help now. The best I can do is declare a nuclear disaster, and look to contain the damage.

With the part of my brain that is still working, I go through a systems check: Am I able to drive? Operating heavy machinery with your head about to go up in a mushroom cloud is never a good idea, but I'm okay with getting home. Going to sleep once I get home, though, is going to be a major problem. My mind is racing far too fast to even think about slowing it down in time for my usual bedtime. Even if I knock myself out with whatever I have in the medicine cabinet, tomorrow is going to be highly problematic. Which means morning will be a complete write-off.

Cycles, wheels within wheels. Had Kraepelin been in the car with me, observing my behavior and asking questions, he would be making a diagnostic coin toss between "depressive or anxious mania" and "agitated depression." Same thing, really—two trains speeding in different directions on the same track. Basically, I'm feeling miserable, but my thoughts and energy levels are in overdrive.

But in a technical sense, I'm still okay. Should I need to fill up my car on the way home, I can at least complete the task without drawing attention to myself. It's just that it may take me a second or two longer to recall my pin number or zip code after I swipe my card. Thinking a zillion unwanted thoughts at once severely compromises my ability to stay in the here and now. Not always, but definitely in times like this. Suddenly, routine mental tasks are no longer routine. Things could be worse.

What's worse? A few weeks later, I would find myself in a Manhattan subway station, sleep-deprived and three thousand miles out of my time zone, unable to locate my MetroCard, not able to find two available neurons to figure out how to get a new card out of one of the machines.

Back to the present: It's not that I am actually in a state of depressive mania or agitated depression, but I'm in mortal danger of heading that way. A good night's sleep, though, will ease me into a soft landing. Thank heaven for sleep. Oh, that's right—I'm in no shape for sleep. The one bipolar fail-safe mechanism for averting disaster only works when there is no impending disaster.

This is why I don't believe in intelligent design, by the way. No manufacturer of the universe with half a brain could have devised an operating system as comically flawed as this.

So now I find myself anticipating the next morning, waking up feeling like Attila the Hun experiencing a mid-life crisis. You really don't want to have me performing brain surgery on you in this state of mind, or for that matter directing your flight into JFK or teaching multiplication tables to your children, or even bagging your groceries.

Fortunately, I work from home and can just declare tomorrow a write-off. Treat my condition as a bad case of the flu. Get plenty of rest. Give it time. Allow my neurons to settle, regroup, my cycles to realign. Then, with an afternoon nap, wake up with my brain reset to nearly normal, good to go.

So here I am, in my car, in wretched condition, but—of all things—able to see into my future with a sense of hope. Such are the workings of self-knowledge.

The unexamined life is not worth living, Socrates famously proclaimed. Socrates also gets credit, along with the Delphic Oracle, as the author of the injunction, "know thyself." In a piece on my blog, *Knowledge is Necessity*, I wrote:

We may have all the book knowledge in the world, all the street knowledge, but the simple fact is all the accumulated wisdom on the planet means nothing without self-knowledge.

In my video introducing readers to my blog, I note:

It's a quest that comes through listening to others and rigorous self-examination. From asking tough questions and grappling with answers we don't necessarily want to hear. ... Often we fail to see how the dots connect. Life is like that. Life, basically, is a first draft. Over time, we acquire wisdom and insight. We become better people. We learn to find a measure of joy and peace of mind. But we also know—nothing is permanent. That life has a way of reducing us to nothing. ...

The circle of life. Cycles-cycles-cycles.

3. FIRST, THE STANDARD VERSION

If you go to the National Institute of Mental Health's (NIMH) website and check out their informational fact sheet on bipolar, you will find no mention of cycles, except in relation to rapid-cycling. Nevertheless, the piece is highly informative. Thus:

Bipolar disorder, also known as manic-depressive illness, is a brain disorder that causes unusual shifts in mood, energy, activity levels, and the ability to carry out daily tasks. Symptoms of bipolar disorder can be severe. They are different from the normal ups and downs that everyone goes through from time to time. Bipolar disorder symptoms can result in damaged relationships, poor job or school performance, and even suicide. But bipolar disorder can be treated, and people with this illness can lead full and productive lives.

If this sounds all too familiar to you, I urge you to skip ahead to the next chapter. But I know for a good many of you, this is your first bipolar book. Trust me, I vividly recall being in your shoes. I will look after you. But whether it's your first book or fiftieth, we all need to start out in the same place, on the same page.

The NIMH goes on to say ...

People with bipolar disorder experience unusually intense emotional states that occur in distinct periods called "mood episodes." Each mood episode represents a drastic change from a person's usual mood and behavior.

To jump in right here: Already, you see the NIMH account deviating from my presentation. It's not that characterizing our illness as "episodic" as opposed to "cyclic" is necessarily wrong. It's just that we're missing the context, the dynamic that drives these episodes and how they relate.

Moving right along …

An overly joyful or overexcited state is called a manic episode, and an extremely sad or hopeless state is called a depressive episode. Sometimes, a mood episode includes symptoms of both mania and depression. This is called a mixed state. People with bipolar disorder also may be explosive and irritable during a mood episode. Extreme changes in energy, activity, sleep, and behavior go along with these changes in mood.

All of this is very much Standard Version. You will find variations on these basic themes everywhere. Indeed, we had this sort of material on display at the DBSA (Depression and Bipolar Support Alliance) support group I used to facilitate back in New Jersey. Not only that, we always had a good supply of NIMH literature in stock. At this level in our education, we don't quibble about the fine points of episodes and cycling. Which is why, if I were facilitating a support group today, I would be happy handing out this same information.

The NIMH goes on to mention a less severe form of mania, known as hypomania. Here …

… you may feel very good, be highly productive, and function well. You may not feel that anything is wrong, but family and friends may recognize the mood swings as possible bipolar disorder. Without proper treatment, people with hypomania may develop severe mania or depression.

The NIMH also lists four main categories of bipolar:

1. Bipolar I — "Defined by manic or mixed episodes, that last at least seven days. ... Usually, depressive episodes occur as well, typically lasting at least 2 weeks."

2. Bipolar II — "Defined by a pattern of depressive episodes and hypomanic episodes, but no full-blown manic or mixed episodes."

3. Bipolar Disorder Not Otherwise Specified [My note: Now called "Other Specified Bipolar and Related Disorders."] — "Diagnosed when symptoms of the illness exist but do not meet diagnostic criteria for either bipolar I or II ..."

4. Cyclothymia — "A mild form of bipolar disorder ..."

We also have a variation referred to as rapid-cycling, characterized by "four or more episodes of major depression, mania, hypomania, or mixed states, all within a year."

The implication to all this is that if you have only felt depressed without at least experiencing some form of mild mania, then you do not have bipolar disorder. Rather, your depression is considered an entirely different disease known as major depressive disorder or its milder variant called persistent depressive disorder (also known as dysthymia). The NIMH has a separate fact sheet for depression.

This book strongly challenges that notion of separation. Instead of the Standard Version, I will ask you to look at depression and bipolar as occupying overlapping bandwidths along the same continuum. Thus, even if you have only experienced depression with no recollection of what it may have been like to feel too good for your own good, there may still be a host of reasons to place you on the "bipolar spectrum."

The reason this is vitally important is that antidepressant medications for "depression" may prove disastrous in your case.

At some point in their presentations, Standard Version accounts reel off depression and mania symptoms, and indeed the NIMH does just that. These are exactly the same, no matter which account you may stumble on. For depression, we have nine symptoms. Checking off at least one from the first two, plus at least four from the next seven (for a total of at least five), and—voila!—depression.

On the "up" side of the equation, the mania and hypomania checklists read exactly the same as each other, word-for-word. The only difference is in severity of symptoms. This time, we have seven symptom items demanding at least three checkmarks.

Make no mistake, these checklists can be most helpful, even validating, for those of us coming to terms with our illness for the first time. Even for those of us experienced in managing our illness, these lists can prove useful in tracking our ever-shifting cycles and adjusting our days accordingly.

But we also need to be mindful how over-reliance on the Standard Version can not only limit understanding and impede recovery, but cause both us and the ones around us to lose sight of our own humanity, leaving us feeling stuck and helpless. We deserve better than that. Much better. Let's investigate …

4. THE DSM: EVOLUTION OF THE STANDARD VERSION

Symptom checklists are the staple of diagnostic psychiatry. These are the work of the American Psychiatric Association (APA), as published in its official bible, the *Diagnostic and Statistical Manual of Mental Disorders, Fifth Edition* (DSM-5), and are replicated everywhere.

The sheer ubiquity of these checklists, though, can be a major problem, especially if you are just trying to pass yourself off as normal. As a general rule, if you're holding down a job it's best to lie low and keep your mouth shut. With a potential love interest, however, you have no choice but to eventually disclose.

Unfortunately, the first thing the would-be love of your life is likely to do is Google "bipolar." Almost instantly, no matter which web page she lands on, out pop the dreaded lists. If the first six items for mania don't send her heading for the hills, the seventh, which reads like a day in the life of a Borgia Pope, certainly will:

Excessive involvement in activities that have a high potential for painful consequences (eg, engaging in unrestrained buying sprees, sexual indiscretions, or foolish business investments).

Cancel that love boat cruise.

Or maybe it's symptom number nine for depression, which comes across as a to-do list in the last day of the life of Anna Karenina:

Recurrent thoughts of death (not just fear of dying), recurrent suicidal ideation without a specific plan, or a suicide attempt or a specific plan for committing suicide.

Try explaining away this to someone you've just met on Match-dot-com.

Nevertheless, as much as we want to disown these aspects of ourselves, we feel our bones resonating in recognition. A certain realization strikes, perhaps born of horror, perhaps relief, probably both. "Oh my God!" you exclaim. That's me. "Thank God!" you exhale. That's me.

Make no mistake: These "Aha!" moments are the first step in our recovery. Listen to anyone successful in managing their bipolar and they will happily relate to you their moment of truth. Nearly every story involves a checklist. Listen further, though, and you will hear accounts of a host of empty feelings that inevitably follow.

"Is this really me?" we find ourselves asking. What about my humanity, my own sense of "normal"? How am I supposed to fit back into my world?

Not too long ago, I found myself trying to explain my condition to a woman I was getting to know. She wanted to find out more, and volunteered she would read up on it.

No! I found myself responding with far greater emphasis than I ever imagined myself capable of. Don't read anything. It's all crap. It will only give you the wrong impression. I repeat, don't read anything.

Not even my own book, I added.

Not even my own book? There it was, *Living Well with Depression and Bipolar Disorder*, sitting in plain sight on my desk. I could have very easily picked it up and handed it to her with a flourish, together with a nice hand-scribbled message.

No, not even my own book, I repeated. And maybe not this one either. Like the evening news, we find ourselves fixating on the train wreck. There is no way of getting

21

around this.

How do I explain? How do I get across the fact that I'm the sum of all of my parts—writer, advocate, granddad, nature boy, music-lover, humanist, geek, dreamer, thinker, joker, mystic—dealing with the same life challenges as everyone else, learning from experience, searching for meaning, finding acceptance, and somehow emerging as a better person, one worth having around?

Just like everyone else. Only I'm more comfortable inside my own normal than someone else's version of normal. In my first book, I thought I had shown how bipolar was a vital part of our true normal. Yet here I was —moment of truth—in mortal fear, pleading with a very lovely and understanding woman not to read it.

Checklists, damned checklists!

Believe it or not, Emil Kraepelin, the man who coined the term manic-depression back in 1899, never came up with a symptom list. To appreciate this, let's begin with his 1921 classic, *Manic-Depressive Insanity*. Manic-depression, he wrote …

… includes on the one hand the whole domain of so-called periodic and circular insanity, on the other hand simple mania, the greater part of the morbid states termed melancholia and also a not inconsiderable number of cases of amentia.

Plus "colorings of mood" that embrace both pathology and personality.

All these diverse elements, claimed Kraepelin, "represent manifestations of a single morbid process." An illness of many faces, in other words, each face connected by a single underlying dynamic—namely cycling. One illness, not five, not 25.

This one-illness concept is crucial to understanding our

condition. The myth about manic-depression is that it is synonymous with bipolar disorder. In the previous chapter, for instance, you may have noticed that even the NIMH's information sheet perpetuated this view. As far as Kraepelin was concerned, however, both clinical depression—what we would later call unipolar depression —and bipolar disorder were both part of manic-depression.

A person could experience depression, in other words, without ever experiencing mania or hypomania and still have manic-depression. This has huge ramifications, which we will get into shortly. What merits our attention right now is that Kraepelin, universally regarded as the father of diagnostic psychiatry, blazed a trail for succeeding generations to explore.

By the time the APA decided to compile a diagnostic bible, however, Freud was the dominant force in psychiatry in the US. The first DSM from 1952 viewed just about all mental illness as some form of adjustment disorder. Thus, the official term for manic-depression was "manic-depressive reaction."

According to the DSM-I, these reactions "are as much determined by inherent personality patterns, the social setting, and the stresses of interpersonal relations as by the precipitating organic impairment."

The DSM-I and its successor, the DSM-II of 1968, actually did preserve the general shape of Kraepelin's manic-depression—including keeping largely intact the one-illness concept—but couldn't resist burying the whole thing in a thick layer of Freudian muck. For instance ...

Neurosis was the Freudian grand organizing principle to explain the behavior of the walking wounded, viewed as psychiatry's meal ticket. "Anxiety" was the driving force of neurosis, which may "be directly felt or expressed" or be "unconsciously and automatically controlled" by various defense mechanisms, such as depression.

You read that right. Depression was a defense mechanism.

Psychiatry's other theory-of-everything came wrapped in "psychosis." The word had a much wider application then than it does today. According to the DSM-II, "mental functioning is sufficiently impaired to interfere grossly with [the patient's] capacity to meet the ordinary demands of life."

Prognosis—hopeless, in other words.

By the time the DSM-II came out in 1968, the public had just about enough of psychiatry. Attacks came from all fronts: Civil liberties activists, victims of psychiatric abuse, the insurance industry, Hollywood, you name it, and naturally from within its own ranks.

Nowhere was this sorry state of affairs made more obvious than in the now-classic Rosenhan study published in *Science* in 1973. Perhaps you've heard of it. This is the experiment where eight healthy subjects were admitted to various psychiatric units after claiming to have heard voices. Seven were given the diagnosis of schizophrenia.

Following admission, the eight behaved normally, but hospital staff interpreted even routine activity as pathological, such as "writing behavior."

In the second part of his experiment, Dr Rosenhan let it be known to a particular hospital that more fake patients were on the way. Ever observant, the hospital weeded out 41 phonies and placed another 42 under suspicion. The joke was on them. All 193 patients were genuine.

According to Dr Rosenhan: "Any diagnostic process that lends itself too readily to massive errors of this sort cannot be a very reliable one."

As if to prove Rosenhan's point, a year later Robert

Spitzer of Columbia University made the case that the situation was even worse than imagined. In an article in the Oct 1974 *British Journal of Psychiatry*, Dr Spitzer reviewed six "reliability" studies across a range of psychiatric diagnoses.

"Reliability" is an indicator of clinician agreement. For instance, if ten radiologists are in accord with the results of the same mammogram, we have a "kappa value" of 1.0. But good luck getting that to happen. Somewhere in the 0.80 range is the best one can expect. A shade north of the 0.20 mark is slightly better than chance.

As for Spitzer's review, for the conditions we regard today as psychiatric, his number-crunching came up with kappa values ranging from .57 to .24. His verdict: "The level of reliability is no better than fair for psychosis and schizophrenia and is poor for the remaining categories."

Spitzer to the rescue. The plot thickens ...

5. THE DSM: HOW THE MOST INFLUENTIAL PSYCHIATRIST NO ONE EVER HEARD OF RESCUED US FROM FREUD

Robert Spitzer began his career as a psychoanalyst, but became disillusioned when hardly any of his patients got better. A chance meeting during the sixties with the head of the DSM-II task force led to a new calling in the academic field of diagnostic psychiatry.

Then came his opportunity to head up the DSM-III. This was a rather dubious undertaking, with no glory, like felling trees in a Zen forest. Psychiatry simply wasn't paying attention.

Back in the seventies, all but a handful of the university psychiatric departments in the US were dominated by Freudians. The exceptions were known as the Mid-Atlantics, which included Washington University in St Louis. (Yes, I know—psychiatrists make terrible geographers.) There, during the fifties and sixties, a trio of science-minded visionaries—Eli Robins, Samuel Guze, and George Winokur—had built their own small parallel universe based on what psychiatry might have looked like had Freud never been born.

Later, as their influence spread, they and their followers would be known as "neo-Kraepelians." Yes, Kraepelin, again. As Dr Guze later recalled, they thought that they "could really make a dent in American psychiatry."

In the meantime, a new era of biological psychiatry was in the making. In 1957, for instance, the Swedish pharmacologist Arvid Carlsson—who would later share a Nobel Prize in Physiology or Medicine—identified dopamine as a neurotransmitter.

As an aside, think of dopamine as the true God particle, as in: "If you think it's God, it's probably dopamine." Same with love. This doesn't mean that God and love aren't true, but we do know that dopamine is.

In 1977, Dr Carlsson published a journal article that speculated that dopamine dysregulation may play a role in schizophrenia. Talking to God, of course, is all well and good. It's when God talks back …

God, in this case, was Freud and his legacy. "Science advances one funeral at a time," said the great physicist Max Planck.

Enter Dr Spitzer on his own mission from God. When he poked his head in the door at Washington University—six times between 1972 and 1974—he found exactly what he was looking for—checklists! These were the product of a resident there, John Feighner. In 1972, the "Feigner Criteria," comprising 16 lists, made its debut in the *Archives of General Psychiatry.*

Dr Feigner and his co-authors—which included the trio of Robins-Guze-Winokur—made it clear that their symptom lists should only be employed as part of a much wider diagnostic exercise involving follow-up visits and family histories and so on. Moreover, they let it be known that their lists were incomplete—basically rough drafts—and that they expected their criteria would change in response to new inputs from other researchers.

As Francis Bacon back in the seventeenth century put it: "Books must follow sciences, and not sciences books."

For depression and mania, the differences between Feigner's lists and today's DSM are minuscule. What turned out to be earth-shaking was how these lists would later be fashioned into a new diagnostic order. "Depression," for instance, was primed to serve double-duty—as an "episode" along with mania under the rubric of "bipolar disorder," and as a separate illness, "major depressive disorder," solely comprising "unipolar" depression.

This, of course, represented a major departure from Kraepelin's original unified view of manic-depression. Yet, there was merit to this new approach. In the 1960s, the German psychiatrist Karl Leonhard had done pioneering work in the field. The American connection was Dr Winokur, also doing pioneering work. Together their research pointed to differences in family background and clinical course.

The term "unipolar" came from two European researchers, Jules Angst and Carlos Perris, making similar observations.

These were exciting times. Dr Spitzer threw himself into his work and mobilized science-minded thinkers from the Mid-Atlantics (including, most notably, Columbia University and Johns Hopkins) to fill 25 committees. The catch was there wasn't much in the way of psychiatric science at the time, but this only lent a sense of higher purpose to the enterprise. The field was wide open to new ideas. Psychiatry was growing up, one exhilarating food fight at a time.

By this time, the Freudians were in retreat, but they still had the strength to severely compromise Spitzer's project. The key to official approval came down to testing the new symptom lists in the field. This had to do with the type of reliability studies and kappa values we talked about at the end of the previous chapter. Thus, if everything worked right, Spitzer could lay some claim to scientific legitimacy.

Basically, if a patient walked in the door babbling a mile-a-minute about how he stayed up all night writing the score to a musical comedy based on the last act to

Shakespeare's *Hamlet*, would the doctors in the room come to a general agreement that they were observing mania rather than, say, psychosis or schizophrenia?

As it turned out, the answer was yes. Spitzer's results showed "far greater reliability than had previously been obtained with DSM-II." In 1979, the DSM-III came up for approval before the APA. A 2005 *New Yorker* profile of Robert Spitzer by Alix Spiegel picks up the account:

People stood up and applauded. Bob's eyes got watery. Here was a group that he was afraid would torpedo all his efforts, and instead he gets a standing ovation.

Another narrative recounts the psychiatric thought leaders of the day singing their high praises. "A fateful point in the history of the American psychiatric profession," enthused the eminent Gerald Klerman, recently retired from his post as the highest-ranking psychiatrist in the federal government.

The DSM-III became an instant runaway success. For the first time, clinicians, researchers, and other stakeholders had a common language. Likewise, patients for the first time could enter a clinician's office with the reasonable expectation of an accurate diagnosis and the appropriate treatment.

If Freud is the person we most associate with psychiatry, then we need to think of Spitzer as the man who drove the final nail into his coffin. More than three decades later, we are still viewing psychiatric illness through a single man's eyes. Whether in the clinic or the research lab—insurance office, congressional hearing, or a patient support group—Spitzer's DSM is the undisputed authority.

Every day, whether it involves reading a page or

clicking a link, consulting with a clinician, influencing public policy, approving a new drug, or figuring out reimbursements, Spitzer continues to touch the lives of millions.

That's one hell of a legacy for someone no one ever heard of.

Thus did Spitzer rescue psychiatry. It makes for one jolly good story, but how well does it hold up? Let's investigate ...

6. THE DSM: BUSTING THE MYTH

I cannot recall what the topic was at a certain dinner symposium at the 2003 American Psychiatric Association annual meeting in San Francisco, or who the speakers were, but I can never forget who grabbed the empty seat next to me. "Robert Spitzer," read his name tag.

Out of deference, I waited for the psychiatrists at the table to open the conversation. I would just be a fly on the wall. But no one spoke. Silence. Just the clinking of glasses and the rattling of plates. I always knew psychiatrists were a bit weird, but this was ridiculous.

I introduced myself to Dr Spitzer as a bipolar patient who was at this particular conference as a journalist. These days, I simply introduce myself as a journalist. Back then, I over-identified with being an entry in Spitzer's diagnostic schema.

Anyway, I had a few thoughts of my own about the DSM, I told Dr Spitzer. Would he be interested in hearing them?

This is like telling Einstein that I had a few thoughts about relativity, but Dr Spitzer indicated that I proceed.

I decided to stick to just one aspect of the DSM. This concerned the issue of gender and depression. My view, which happened to echo those of a host of credible experts, was that the DSM symptom list is biased toward picking up depression in women while men suffer in silence. According to conventional wisdom, twice as many women experience depression as men. But a bit of tweaking to that symptom list, I argued, could even out that equation.

Then I rattled off four symptoms that I felt needed

fixing.

Dr Spitzer pondered my comments. Then, as psychiatrists are wont to do, said nothing. By now, the main course had come out. Any further conversation was light and inconsequential. Soon the first of several speakers started talking. It was time to go to work, to take notes.

Two hours later, the last of the speakers wrapped up. Question time was just ahead. Most members of the audience use this brief interval to leave, and so it was that Dr Spitzer got up to make his exit, but not before addressing me.

"I thought about what you said," he told me, or words to that effect. And then his verdict: "And I don't go along with any of it."

Then he rose from his chair and was gone. Poof! No chance for me to even say, thank you for putting up with me.

Reading Spitzer's profile in the *New Yorker* two years later gave me an insight into the man's table manners. According to the piece, success went to his head. He became adamant about his opinions and made enemies:

"A lot of what's in the DSM represents what Bob thinks is right," Michael First, a psychiatrist at Columbia who worked on both the DSM-III-R and DSM-IV, says. "He really saw this as his book, and if he thought it was right he would push very hard to get it in that way."

Spitzer's main collaborator, Jean Endicott of Columbia University, observed that he didn't seem to grasp other people all that well, and displayed surprise whenever he learned that he had annoyed someone.

Basically, Spitzer was a genius visionary turned

anachronistic grouch, a Henry Ford who fell in love with his Model T. But the fault was not his alone. As it happened, the spectacular success of the DSM turned out to be its greatest failure. Once everyone bought into the document—the entire clinical-research-Pharma-insurance industrial complex, basically—it was virtually impossible to change it.

Thus, in complete violation of Bacon, science now followed the book.

By this time, according to the *New Yorker* profile, just about everyone was complaining about Spitzer's table manners. This cost him his chance to head up the DSM-IV of 1994. The new chair, Allen Frances of Duke University, put his committees on notice to cut back on "the wild growth and casual addition" of new mental disorders. In a piece published in the June 29, 2009 *Psychiatric Times*, Dr Frances appeared to be bragging about how little he actually accomplished:

In the subsequent evolution of descriptive diagnosis, DSM-III-R and DSM-IV were really no more than footnotes to DSM-III ...

The DSM-5 of 2013, led by David Kupfer of the University of Pittsburgh, took the same conservative approach. The year prior to publication, the DSM-5 had released the findings from its own reliability studies. Recall that "reliability" is an indicator of clinician agreement, as measured in kappa values. Spitzer based the scientific legitimacy of his DSM-III on stellar results from his own reliability trials. These results represented a quantum leap over the "fair to poor" outcomes he had uncovered in the DSM-II.

Get ready, drumroll ...

The DSM-5 turned in kappa values well below those

from both the DSM-III and DSM-IV eras and in the same range as the ones from the bad old days of the DSM-II. You read that right. The latest version of the DSM failed to outperform the antiquated and much-maligned DSM-II

What gives? The only explanation that makes sense is that Spitzer's research was bogus. More damning, no one at the time seemed to have taken the trouble to either vet his findings or demand that he publish more detailed data. A 1992 account by University of California sociologists Stuart Kirk and Herb Kutchins goes into this in great detail. The bottom line is that scientific rigor took an extended leave of absence.

So it was that three decades passed before Spitzer's successors accidentally but most definitively busted him. Robert Spitzer, hero or huckster? Both, actually. Life is complicated.

In the meantime, the show must go on. Thus, after a lot of hemming and hawing, in an editorial in the Jan 2012 *American Journal of Psychiatry*, Dr Kupfer and other members of the DSM-5 task force interpreted their reliability results as "realistic" and "acceptable."

Alas, how about credible?

Okay, let's pause here for a second. I have no interest in exposing the workings of psychiatry's evil empire or its partner-in-crime, the pharmaceutical industry. Both the internet and mainstream publishing already well-serve this particular market need. Indeed, much of the commentary is eye-opening and well worth reading. Even better, you will feel a sense of empowerment.

But when all is said and done, you still have your bipolar to contend with. It's there. It lives inside your brain. It's not going to go away. Somehow, we need to learn to live with it, come to terms, find our own ways of coping, and of finding meaning in our lives. Singling out villains only goes so far. At the end of the day, we—all of us—need to figure out how to be our own heroes. This is where the real empowerment lies.

So let's reframe this whole discussion. The best way to do that is rewind to my unexpected dinner with Robert Spitzer. As you recall, our conversation came in the course of a dinner symposium at the 2003 American Psychiatric Association (APA) annual meeting. This was a gathering of about 20,000 psychiatrists and other mental health professionals which took place at the Moscone Center and nearby hotel ballrooms in San Francisco over a six-day period.

Let's step out into the fresh air …

7. THE DSM: KILLING BUDDHA

A spring afternoon, the APA annual meeting, San Francisco, 2003: I headed out of the Moscone Center to my next seminar, taking place at nearby hotel. I fell in line with a group of attendees headed the same way. At an intersection, we were held up by antipsychiatry protestors parading down the street, making noise and waving signs saying, "Psychiatry kills." At the time, the antipsychiatry movement was attracting media notice by going on hunger strikes and by issuing public challenges to the APA to prove that mental illness existed.

According to the intellectual father of antipsychiatry, the late Thomas Szasz, himself a psychiatrist, mental illness is not real.

I waited until the crowd passed, then made my way to my next round of PowerPoint presentations, where the real assault on conventional psychiatry was taking place.

"The DSM-IV was not designed with human gene function in mind, and genes do not code for psychopathology," I heard Robert Freedman of the University of Colorado explain to us. Over the years, to the delight of numerous professional audiences, I would hear many variations on this theme from numerous other speakers.

Good luck finding a depression or bipolar or schizophrenia gene, in other words. Dr Freedman was tracking a promising lead that had to do with why those with schizophrenia smoked so much. The trail led to a neural malfunction in certain people in their ability to filter out noise in their environment. This has major implications for bipolar, as well.

In the meantime, other researchers were chasing down stress, which you could find at the scene of nearly every brain-related crime. This is the conference, by the way, where I first learned to correctly pronounce "amygdala." This is the part of the brain that kicks off the fight-or-flight response, and fresh studies were rolling in.

In another dark room, before another PowerPoint, Daniel Weinberger of the NIMH explained how, in a study, in response to negative stimuli, this part of the brain lit up in people with a certain gene variation. This result corresponded to a contemporaneous population study that showed that individuals with this exact same gene variation were far more likely to get depressed when subjected to stressful events.

Basically, as I would hear Dr Weinberger say at another APA gathering, our genes are all about how we respond to whatever life happens to throw our way. It's not genes vs environment, then. It's environment acting on genes, and vice-versa. And a good deal of the time, stress is the go-between.

Connect the dots from Freedman to Weinberger and a picture begins to emerge of an overwhelmed brain blindly reacting rather than cogently responding. It's a scene that both cuts across numerous diagnostic boundaries and blurs them, from anxiety to autism to bipolar to borderline personality disorder to depression to panic to PTSD to schizophrenia.

The variations are numerous, but the final acts play out with tragic regularity: We lose control. We flip out or shut down. The people around us start pointing fingers. In an effort to cope, we take up unhealthy or questionable behaviors—from abusing alcohol and drugs to going into social isolation to lashing out at those close to us, to engaging in risky pleasures.

If you listen closely, of all things, you can detect faint but clear echoes of those ancient DSMs I and II. Back then, our illnesses were regarded as "maladaptions" to our environment, "reactions" to stress. Mental illness was messy, not fitting into any clear-cut categories—thoughts and behaviors bleeding into other thoughts and behaviors, merging into personality, changing over time, with no clear cut-offs between sick and normal.

Just like the real world. Of all the crazy things, "manic-depressive reaction" and even "neurosis" and depression as a "defense mechanism" begin to make sense. Take a look at the insane world we live in. We weren't built for this. Everyone has a breaking point.

So—are you depressed because you have reached the realization that there is no way you are going to meet your deadlines at work and you have come to the entirely reasonable conclusion that life is hopeless? Or are you flipping into mania because you have stayed up three nights straight trying to meet those same stupid work deadlines?

Or have all those infernal cycles in your head taken on a life of their own?

But who has time for checking into all of that? Especially when our psychiatrists can work off of symptom checklists and see upwards of 1,200 patients a month with no adequate follow-up and call it treatment. But don't take my word for it. This from Nancy Andreasen, one of the world's preeminent psychiatric researchers, in a January 2007 piece in the *Schizophrenia Bulletin*:

Since the publication of DSM-III in 1980, there has been a steady decline in the teaching of careful clinical evaluation that is targeted to the individual person's problems and social context and that is enriched by a good general knowledge of psychopathology.

In her piece, Dr Andreasen mourns the loss of observational wisdom, what she calls "phenomenology," a tradition that began with the scientific revolution of the seventeenth century but that you can trace back to ancient Greece. These were your natural philosophers who operated with only minimal aid of scientific instruments, but who compensated with an insanely obsessional eye to detail.

Think of Mendel with his peas or Darwin with his finches. Now think of their ability to generalize their observations into more than just peas and finches.

Hold that thought ...

There is an old Buddhist saying that goes: If you meet the Buddha on the road, kill him.

Basically, anyone who claims the knowledge and authority of a Buddha can only be regarded as a fraud. No one owns the map to reality. At best we are connecting dots across vast unknowns.

In May 2013, just weeks prior to the publication of the DSM-5, Thomas Insel, head of the NIMH, made it official—he killed Buddha. In his Director's Blog, he announced that the NIMH "would be re-orienting its research away from DSM categories." The DSM, he wrote, may be regarded as a "bible in its field," but at best, it is a "dictionary, creating a set of labels and defining each." According to Dr Insel: "Patients with mental disorders deserve better."

No kidding.

In future books, we will be giving this matter a lot more attention and steering the conversation toward what Nobel Laureate Eric Kandel describes as "the new science of the mind," one that would fold Freud into neurobiology. We will also be taking the discussion a lot wider and deeper, which involves paying attention to a far broader range of experts.

In addition, we will be expanding our horizons to our higher expectations in life. In essence, "knowing thyself" is a quest that will take us from God to neurons.

But we need to begin with that dying breed of those keepers of the observational wisdom that Dr Andreasen referred to. Thus, in this book—stage one in our journey —we will be hearing a lot from Frederick Goodwin, former head of the NIMH and co-author with Kay Jamison of *Manic-Depressive Illness*, Hagop Akiskal of UCSD, foremost proponent of the bipolar spectrum, and the Zurich-based psychiatrist Jules Angst. These are men well past retirement age, who trace their lineage back to Emil Kraepelin.

I am also indebted to the work of the late Greek psychiatrist, Athanasios Koukopoulos, who once reminded a younger psychiatrist that Hippocrates' clinical acuity and understanding of human diseases derived from the fact that he was first and foremost a poet.

In addition, Kay Jamison, Dr Goodwin's co-author, a baby-boomer from my generation, brings an unparalleled literary sensibility to her clinical observations. Then there is the younger Nassir Ghaemi of Tufts University, who learned under Dr Goodwin and acquired a graduate philosophy degree to go with his MD and MPH.

Trust me, the humanities greatly inform the scientist.

I will make every attempt to represent the work of these and other clinical observers as fairly and accurately as possible, but I reserve the right to connect my own dots, fly off on my own tangents, and draw my own conclusions.

Further on in this book, I introduce a different set of experts into the narrative—bloggers and memoir-writers with whom I've enjoyed a close and valued association over the years.

Hopefully, as a picture begins to emerge, you will recognize bits and pieces of yourself. You will connect your own dots, form your own conclusions, call your own shots. There are many paths to recovery, but everything begins with knowing thyself. Onward …

8. PERSONALITY AND TEMPERAMENT

Socrates, help me out. Here I am, in my car, facing the aftermath of a disastrous meeting, about to go up in a Chernobylic plume of radioactive dust. In Chapter Two, we looked at what might be going on from a mood perspective, but that is only half the picture.

The other half has to do with personality and temperament. The bipolar literature consistently ignores this, but not Kraepelin. In his 1921 *Manic-Depressive Insanity*, he saw "colorings of mood" as passing "without sharp boundary into the domain of personal predisposition."

In fact, Kraepelin put a lot of thought into this. Under the heading of "personal idiosyncrasy," he viewed depression as arising out of a depressive temperament, though in rare cases mania may emerge. The same dynamic applied to mania arising from a manic disposition.

Then there are those in-between temperaments he defined as "irritable" and "cyclothymic," where anything was likely to happen.

Thus, the tension between "state"—a temporary condition identified with our illness—and "trait"— something that defines our personality and which will remain fairly constant our entire lives. Each exerts a sort of magnetic attraction and repulsion on the other. Both, in turn, are buffeted by those shifting forces we call our environment.

I first heard Hagop Akiskal expound on the topic to an overflowing session at the 2002 American Psychiatric Association annual meeting in Philadelphia. A lot of it was literally Greek to me. Seriously, he talked about the ancient Greeks. At first, I thought this had to be the introduction to his presentation, but no—this was his whole talk and I barely understood a word of it.

It was only much later—years, in fact—that the light came on, and when it did my understanding became three-dimensional. So bear with me. What I'm about to relate may seem a bit mystifying, at first. But I will walk you through it every step of the way. Don't feel you have to understand everything right now. Trust me, in later chapters, the pieces will fall into place.

Okay, let's proceed …

The ancient Greeks gave the world their version of yin-yang in the form of the four humors. It was all about balance and harmony. A good "temperament" signified a "correct mixture." If you had too much of one thing, "sanguine"—representing a beating heart nourished by the liver—was the way to go. "Choler" and "phlegmatic" had clear downsides.

Then we come to "melancholia," which literally means black bile. We know what that is like. The Greeks believed that this particular essence bubbled up from the spleen, but other things were also involved—the element earth, the season winter, old age, and the planet Saturn. Think of melancholia as a cold and dry state.

Thus, according to Galen the Physician: "The mind's inclination follows the body's temperature."

Okay, bear with me for a second. I'm about to introduce Shakespeare into the picture. Yes, I know, just what you need, a reminder of high school English classes. But nowhere can we find the four humors on better display. Our favorite Bard even devoted an entire tragedy to a certain melancholic Dane.

Thus, Gertrude to her son: "Good Hamlet, cast thy

nighted color off."

Easier said than done, of course, when forced to tread lightly in the presence of a murderous stepfather, "in his retirement, marvelous distempered ... with choler."

Contemplate the spectacle of our title character, prone to soliloquistic ruminations, questioning his own sanity, attributing his confusion to a state arising "out of my weakness and my melancholy."

By the way, the Bard used the word earth—melancholy's special element—and its variants 23 times in the play. As in: "Though all the earth o'erwhelm them, to men's eyes."

The ancient Greeks did not include references to the elements and seasons and planets and so on for mere literary purposes. My spleen may well be inclined to spew too much black bile, but other forces are also at play, which exert a tempering—or distempering—effect. Thus, we are subject to changing circumstances—earth, air, fire, water—forced to adapt and adjust. And yet again, we are victims of our own birth, legatees of those mysterious heavenly forces that stay with us till the day we die.

Recall in Chapter Two how I had Kraepelin in the car with me and how he came to the conclusion that I was either dealing with a "depressive or anxious mania" or "agitated depression." In either case, a mixed state, two moods manifesting at once. Now I have Galen the Physician by my side. Of all things, he makes the same diagnosis—two moods, two biles, black and yellow.

Imagine Shakespeare tagging along and interpreting this as a melancholic choler.

But what is the true status of my respective biles? Is my melancholy a true expression of my personality? A condition that implies a sense of permanence? Or is it something fleeting? A cold dry wind from Saturn.

Temperament or illness? Perhaps both? What about my choler? To be gone when the hot wind from Mars stills?

Let's bring Kraepelin back for a consultation. He and Galen are nodding in agreement. Different terminology, similar analysis.

Now Socrates steps into the picture. It's all about knowing thyself. Otherwise, bipolar is an empty label. Otherwise, how we think and feel and behave will always remain a mystery. It's a never-ending quest. But I am in no shape to get to the bottom of it right now. It's been a long hard day. Shakespeare leans forward and reassuringly pats me on the shoulder. "O sleep!" he says. "O gentle sleep! Nature's soft nurse."

9. IS IT NORMAL OR IS IT BIPOLAR?

Never underestimate the healing power of sleep. The catch is, when I wake up I want to feel myself, but not necessarily normal. Kraepelin isn't much help, here. Unfortunately, neither are the people charged with treating us.

Back in 2008, I gave my first and last grand rounds ever. Grand rounds is a fancy name for a giving a talk to doctors. This one was to a group of about 50 clinicians at a psychiatric hospital in Princeton, New Jersey. "Keep in mind," I said, "a lot of us view the world through the eyes of artists and poets and visionaries and mystics. Not to mention through the eyes of highly successful professionals and entrepreneurs. We don't want to be like you."

Kelvin grade frozen stony cold silence. I couldn't help but think: Why is what I'm saying so strange to these people? Why are they just sitting there, not reacting? Had I been an experienced speaker, I would have thrown away my script and initiated a dialogue. Instead, I blurted out: "To me, you all have flat affect" (ie lack of expression).

And that was the part of my talk that went over reasonably well, mind you. Thirty minutes later, the second my lips stopped moving, they were out the door. I never knew it was possible to empty a room so fast.

Here's the deal: Kraepelin was the master observer, but he limited his inquiry to patients in asylums, which badly skewed his sample. Suppose, in addition, he had taken in clients off the street. Imagine his contemporary, the celebrated conductor and composer Gustav Mahler walking into his office.

No other classical composer elicits the kind of cult

following, gives you the sense of belonging to a special club, more than Mahler. His music has that effect. According to the conductor Leonard Bernstein:

Basically, of course, all of Mahler's music is about Mahler—which means simply that it is about conflict. ... Mainly the battle rages between Western Man at the turn of the century and the life of the spirit. Out of this opposition proceeds the endless list of antitheses—the whole roster of Yang and Yin—that inhabit Mahler's music.

An early partner of Mahler's said that living with him was "like being on a boat that is ceaselessly rocked to and fro by the waves." He eventually married a beautiful socialite, Alma, 19 years younger. A falling out sent him into family therapy—with Sigmund Freud, no less. Really, you can't make this stuff up.

Kraepelin and Freud were born the same year. Both laid down the groundwork for all of psychiatry to follow. But suppose, back in 1910, it had been Kraepelin, not Freud, probing Mahler's mind.

Mahler described himself as three times homeless—a Bohemian in Austria, an Austrian among Germans, and a Jew throughout the world. Throw in a little bit crazy to make that four times homeless. Add in one more helping of homeless, for good measure.

Still, we are talking about a man who nailed every conceivable success benchmark and then some, including landing the most prestigious conducting gig in Europe—director of the Vienna Court Opera. Would that have given Kraepelin food for thought?

Kay Jamison, in her 1996 book *Touched with Fire*, speculates that Mahler was dealing with cyclothymia, a form of bipolar lite, rather than the full-blown version. It's not hard to see her reasoning: He didn't drink himself into oblivion like Beethoven. He didn't jump off a bridge into the Rhine like Schumann.

Nor did he do anything spectacularly strange like Van Gogh.

But one can only speculate what could have happened had not his heart given out on him first, at the age of 50, especially with suicide running in his family. Until 1907, Mahler's pattern had been to alternate between his hectic life in Vienna and extended time-outs in the Alps, where he got out in nature and composed at leisure.

Then things changed. In the space of a few months, he resigned his post at the Opera, his young daughter died, and he was diagnosed with a severe heart condition. Then he became a wanderer, back and forth between New York and Europe. In 1910—a year before his death—he discovered his wife was having an affair. That's when he sought out Freud.

Here's Bernstein commenting on the eerily subdued finale to his musical swan song, his *Ninth Symphony*: "It's as if he is trying on for size disembodiment."

So what would Kraepelin have made of all that? In 1910, the man who came up with the term manic-depression was a professor of clinical psychiatry at the University of Munich. In that very city, that same year, Mahler premiered his *Eighth Symphony*, popularly known as the *Symphony of a Thousand*. Typically, his strange works mystified his listeners. This time, though, following a short pause, the audience erupted in a rapturous ovation lasting twenty minutes.

Suppose Kraepelin had been in that audience, in a venue just down the road from his place of work, hearing Mahler on the composer's own terms, a witness to his greatest triumph. How would that have influenced his then-evolving perception of manic-depressive insanity?

Let's be clear on this: The diagnosis of bipolar isn't a merit badge. I'm writing this and you are reading this because at some point in our existence our lives turned into a catastrophic train wreck. And there we were, some time later, trembling, head in hands, vaguely responding to a psychiatrist's questions, wondering how the hell we were supposed to pick up the pieces.

Maybe some of you are feeling that way right now. Hopefully, you will find this book helpful. But the point of this book is different than the one I wrote back in 2006, namely: Knowing our illness makes no sense without knowing ourselves. It's not enough to assume that once we get our bipolar under control that we can simply navigate our way back to normal. Especially if we have no concept of our own true normal.

This is especially true, having regard for the fact that our condition is so embedded in our personality and subject to the whims of our environment. Over the years I have learned to accept the fact that I will be more depressed than I would like to be and more animated than those around me would like me to be.

There will also be those times I find myself alone and isolated, questioning my very existence and freaking out and falling to pieces over nothing. And when this happens there is nothing more I would rather do than remove my infinitely unreliable brain from its casing and return it to the customer service counter of life.

I wouldn't even ask the clerk to replace it with a brain that works. Stuff anything into the empty space. Bubble-wrap, pie filling—I'm fine with that. Then, on reflection, I can't help but think: You know, most people have already chosen those options. Do I really want to be like them? Pie filling for brains? Normal?

Do you?

"That is the question," Shakespeare lets me know. We are back in my car. I have a long drive home ahead of me. My good buddy reaches over and turns on the radio to a classical station. Ah, Mahler …

10. BIPOLAR - HERE WE ARE, THIS IS WHAT WE PUT UP WITH, BUT WHERE THE HELL DID IT COME FROM?

I devote one section of my website, mcmanweb.com, to my own personal stories. The first four track my life from boyhood to early manhood—from when I first started feeling different at age six to feelings of being alone against the world six years later and on to my early depressions and teen insecurities to my first crash and burn in college.

There is a certain sense of inevitability to the narrative, as if I were doomed from the get-go. Picking up the account at the beginning of my fourth article:

If you have ever read news accounts of airlines that crashed, you will inevitably find they were doomed to crash. Sleet build-up on the wings, a five-cent bolt that worked its way loose, a runway that was too short for the conditions at hand— ou get the picture. The pilot taxies into position, gets the all-clear from the control tower, and races down the strip, fully expecting to become airborne, taking comfort in the roar of four Pratt and Whitney engines outside his cockpit, blithely ignorant of the fatal defect that will put him and his passengers in the bottom of a swamp.

I wrote these pieces in a white heat in early 1999, at age 49, very soon after I was diagnosed following a lifetime of denial. My diagnosis changed everything. It forced me to come to a sense of acceptance with the present, and once that happened my past suddenly made sense. For the first time, I could talk about my childhood.

But at the time, I simply saw these pieces as foreshadowing. You either had bipolar or you didn't—

that was the state of my thinking back then. It was like pregnancy. You couldn't be just a little bit pregnant. Or could you? And if you could—be a little bit bipolar, that is —could that little bit, over time, snowball into something more significant?

Could I, in effect, by rewinding my life and hitting Play, observe my bipolar slowly revealing itself from distant classrooms and playgrounds? It wasn't long before I came across scattered studies concerning "prodromal" symptoms in children, and suddenly I realized my narrative had a clear story arc.

Prodromal relates to the early warning signs of an illness, such as that scratchy throat prior to the outbreak of a cold. In the context of bipolar, we can often spot depression or anxiety or mania before it happens. We may catch ourselves, for instance, neglecting our personal hygiene or talking too fast or losing our patience around people. With practice, once we learn to spot our own personal signs, we can work to head off an impending episode before it happens, or at least mitigate its worst effects.

This, of course, represents life as usual with a cycling illness. But could prodromal also have something to do with a much larger cycle, one that spans the years and decades—a bipolar life-cycle? In 1994, a research team led by Janice Egeland of the University of Miami recruited a population of healthy Amish youth—one sample from parents known to have bipolar I, the other a control group —and tracked them over the years.

In 2003, the team published their first findings, which showed the kids of bipolar parents at twice the risk of bipolar compared to the control group. Moreover, certain symptoms were more evident in the at-risk group, including anxiety, distractibility and excitability, mood changes, and sleep problems. This strongly suggested bipolar in the making, revealing its first signs at an early age and progressing in intensity over the years until we ultimately come across behavior clearly recognizable as bipolar.

But until fairly recently, we had no grand unifying theory. That changed for me in 2009, on a brilliant spring morning, while having a coffee and a bagel out on the terrace of the San Diego Convention Center. Someone sat down across from me and gave me the equivalent of a master class.

The International Congress on Schizophrenia Research was about to begin its second or third day. Over breakfast, Beatriz Luna of the University of Pittsburgh told me she wasn't a schizophrenia researcher. Rather, her specialty concerned something called "development." As in child psychology? I asked.

No, she told me. This was about brain development, as in the child brain maturing into the adult brain. Adolescence, she informed me, involves major risk of mental illness. This is when the brain changes gears. But what if something goes wrong in the transition? Might this underlie the pathology of mental illness?

Knock me over with a feather.

Quick aside: The bipolar experts could benefit from talking to their counterparts in schizophrenia. Sadly, they don't. As a result, those in the field often come across as operating in an isolated research backwater, only talking amongst themselves. So it was that I nearly burst into song when at this same conference I ran into Carrie Bearden of UCLA. I had corresponded with her in the past, and our paths had crossed at previous bipolar conferences. Call it coincidence, call it whatever you want, several years later I happened to come across a transcript of a talk she gave in 2013, one that essentially built on Dr Luna, but from a bipolar perspective.

Here is the basic story …

During adolescence, the brain loses about 40 percent of its cortical synapses. There is an actual loss of grey matter. In a child's brain, there are excessive connections, so this synaptic (or dendritic) pruning is normal.

In addition to grey matter changes, there are also white matter changes. White matter connects different regions of grey matter. These are basically thread-like neural axons insulated in a fatty myelin sheath. Through a process of myelination, these connections grow stronger, allowing the brain to process information and perform tasks more efficiently.

All well and good. The catch is that the different brain regions don't all develop at the same time. It appears that the reactive subcortical and limbic areas mature first, and become, in effect, entirely too efficient. Hence the phenomenon of the teen-ager.

At the same time, during adolescence, there are circadian changes in the brain, regulated by the suprachiasmatic nucleus (SCN) located behind the eye. Dr Bearden asks us to think of the SCN as "the conductor of an orchestra," responsible for the homeostatic processes in regulating sleep and wakefulness and a host of other vital functions.

Now a picture begins to emerge of all the things that can go wrong when our adolescent operating system fails to make its scheduled upgrades. If our full cortical and homeostatic capacities fail to come online, our ability to regulate our sleep and behavior, respond to stress, plan ahead, and reign in impulses is going to be severely compromised.

This helps explain my early life story—and yours. Pause

for a second and consider:

Maybe somehow, despite everything, you managed to scrape through high school with decent enough grades to get into college. Here, though, it may have all caught up with you. Combine a vulnerable brain with a drastic change in environment, and next thing, mid-semester, your parents are driving you home.

Or maybe it all blew up on you when you hit the work force. Life transitions are killers. That dream entry-level job, the one with zilch pay and high pressure and 100-hour weeks, how did that one turn out?

An ongoing study by Anne Duffy of the University of Calgary validates our experiences. Back in the early 2000s, she and her colleagues recruited 229 children who had one bipolar parent and tracked them for up to 16 years. Although these children constituted a high-risk population, the vast majority did not develop bipolar. Of those who did, clear patterns emerged, in a series of stages, namely:

During childhood, we see well states punctuated by non-mood disturbances, such as anxiety and sleep. Into adolescence, we find minor mood disturbances and adjustment issues. Later, we see major depression breaking out. Indeed, eight in ten of those in the study who developed bipolar began with a depressive episode. Mania—if it does eventuate—tends not to show its face till late teen/early adulthood.

In a later chapter, we will discuss neuroplasticity and why the situation isn't hopeless. This was also a topic that was featured at the schizophrenia conference I attended, but one I invariably fail to encounter at bipolar conferences. But for the time being, in case you've been wondering all your life how you got this way, well now you have a credible explanation.

This is part of our quest to know thyself. Maybe now, for the first time ever, your life is starting to make sense. If so, we can journey further.

11. THE MAP TO REALITY

Yes, I know, I know. In Chapter Seven, I flat-out stated that no one owns the map to reality, but I came up with this one myself and I'm going with it:

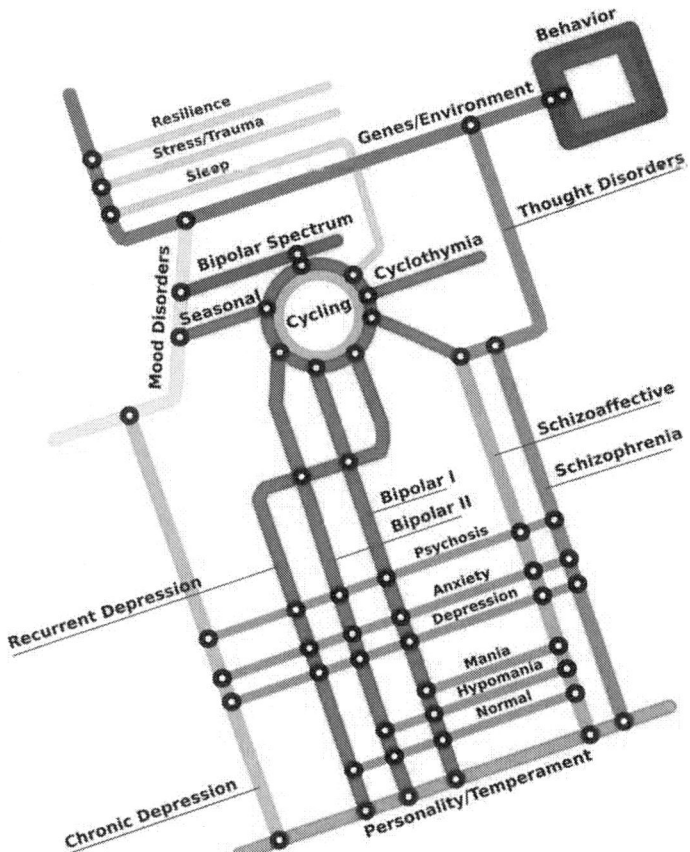

It might be fun to recall what you read in the earlier chapters and see how your understanding corresponds with the map. Then see if you can connect your own dots. At this stage, we are simply establishing a broad overview. Note, for instance, the connections between temperament and various mood states at the bottom, then how the bipolar tracks feed into cycling in the middle—or cycling feeds into bipolar.

Then check out the top part of the map, which has to do with the new science of the mind. Note how top, bottom, and middle connect. Finally, observe how everything in the end feeds into behavior—or, in reverse, how behavior feeds into everything.

Everything, in essence, is influencing everything. The trains are running in both directions and many trains are running at once.

Don't worry if the map looks overwhelming. In upcoming chapters, we will walk you through it, step by step. But one thing you won't find on this map is home. First things first—we need to orient ourselves, figure out where we are right now, how we got here, and where we may be headed. Only then will we begin to recognize the signs pointing the way home. And that's a map you will wind up drawing yourself.

This wraps up Part I. To summarize:

We need to think of bipolar as a cycling illness, with the brain constantly in flux. We also need to view our illness as existing along a spectrum with a clear relationship to unipolar depression. This is closer in accord to how Emil Kraepelin described manic-depression back in the early twentieth century.

To this day, no one has surpassed Kraepelin's powers of observation. In the US, however, his legacy was hijacked by Freud and his disciples. The American Psychiatric

Association's DSMs I and II from the fifties and sixties preserved the general structure of Kraepelin's manic-depression, but essentially buried it under the Freudian muck of neurosis and maladaptations.

The publication of Spitzer's DSM-III in 1980 proved a watershed moment in psychiatry. But in the process, clinicians lost sight of the true nature of our condition. Overnight, bipolar became narrowly defined and reduced to symptom checklists. One unintended consequence was that of true bipolars being misdiagnosed with unipolar depression and put on the wrong meds.

As it turned out, the DSM-III and its successors failed to live up to their hype. In the meantime, DSM psychiatry came under assault from a variety of fronts, most notably from new advances in brain science.

The brain science has had the effect of blurring diagnostic boundaries. Rather than starting with clusters of symptoms and searching for whatever biology may lie underneath, researchers at the NIMH and other centers are urging us to reverse the order of our inquiry, to instead focus on brain circuits, which influence our ability to process inputs from the environment, including our buried memories. Our stress response is an important part of this equation. Ironically, folding in stress may force us to reconsider Freud.

We also raised the issue of "normal." In one context, normal represents those lucid intervals in between our mood states. But when we factor personality and temperament into the equation, we recognize that no longer can we take normal for granted.

Finally, we gave you the opportunity to look back on your life, to see what may have been going on during the innocence of your child and teen years, when you guessed something may not have been right, but you had no idea what.

At every step of the way, we encouraged you to know yourself. Simply knowing about our illness is not enough. Reality can be a strange place, but once we get our bearings, once we get a sense of who we are, we are set to journey home.

PART TWO: MAPPING MOOD

Do not swear by the moon, for she changes constantly ...

—Shakespeare, Romeo and Juliet

12. THE BIPOLAR SPECTRUM AND RECURRENCE

It's amazing how simplicity and elegance can underlie complexity and chaos. We see this in Einstein's $E=MC^2$, Watson and Crick's DNA double helix, and Darwin's theory of natural selection. With bipolar, the answer is staring us right in the face—we are looking at a cycling phenomenon.

Recall that back in 1851 Falret came up with circular insanity and that Kraepelin saw both depression and mania as part of the same illness, one that embraced periodic and circular insanity. The illness was "recurrent" in nature. In other words those depressions and manias kept returning. In this sense, "normal" was part of the disease process, those lucid intervals between episodes.

"Polarity" did not matter to Kraepelin. As Athanasios Koukopoulos and his co-authors point out in an editorial in the July 2013 *British Journal of Psychiatry*, if a patient had ten consecutive depressions, it was manic-depression. If he or she had ten consecutive manias, it was manic-depression.

Goodwin and Jamison, in their second edition of *Manic-Depressive Illness,* note that the modern shift to polarity discourages clinicians from thinking in terms of cyclicity and recurrence. As a result, they fail to see the illness for the episode.

Recurrence and cycling are not limited to bipolar. According to Goodwin and Jamison, these are the hallmarks of one-third or more of those with so-called unipolar depression, what they call "highly recurrent" depression. These are individuals in the course of experiencing at least their fourth depression. No manias, no hypomanias.

So, imagine being visited by your second depression in a row. Conventional psychiatry would have us disregard that first depression and not recognize the strong possibility of a third. Goodwin and Jamison and others, in effect, ask us to connect the dots, to link these supposedly separate episodes together. This is especially true when we consider that a second depression raises the likelihood of a third one occurring to 80 percent.

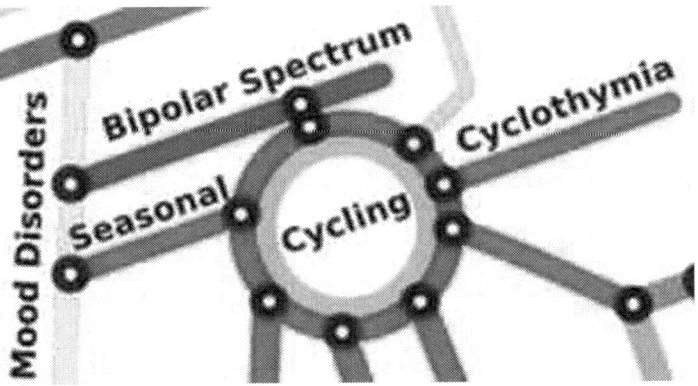

Map of reality close-up 1: Cycling, not polarity, is what drives every condition occurring along the bipolar spectrum. Seen from this light, we need to regard recurrent depression as bearing a close relationship to bipolar I and bipolar II, as represented by the three vertical red lines at the bottom of the image.

This section of the map also reveals the extremes in cycling. The thin bent line running to the top represents sleep, which is part of our daily circadian cycle, and—of course—the gradual turning of the seasons.

Essentially, people who experience recurrent depressions cycle up to "normal" rather than manic or hypomanic. In this regard, "normal" can be considered part of the disease process, an interlude between depressive episodes. This begs the obvious question: Shouldn't this depressed population be properly regarded as bipolar? We already have a bipolar I and bipolar II. Why not a bipolar III?

This is more or less the position—with major qualifications—advanced by Hagop Akiskal and Nassir Ghaemi. Goodwin and Jamison, on the other hand, favor keeping the name recurrent depression, but stressing its kinship to bipolar.

The issue involves what Plato called "carving nature at its joints." This gets entirely problematic if the entity in question has no joints. According to Oregon psychiatrist Jim Phelps, writing in a chapter of a collaborative academic text on bipolar II, there should be zones of rarity between two similar but distinct species.

To freely interpret, out in nature, we are not likely to come across a creature resembling a rhinopotamus. But can the same be said for mood disorders?

To understand what is going on, we need to conceptualize bipolar and a good deal of unipolar depression in terms of overlapping conditions along a continuous spectrum. Dimensions, not categories. The easiest way to grasp this is by examining the diagram below. What we are looking at is the pattern of an individual cycling in and out of depression. Note, in all three representations, the depressions are exactly the same.

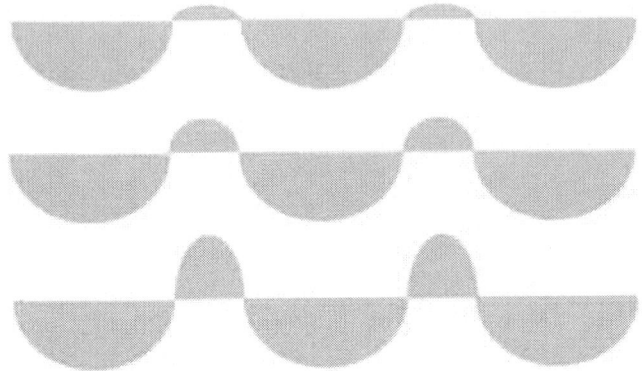

The top representation illustrates recurrent unipolar depression, separated by intervals of "normal." The middle representation more closely resembles bipolar II, with the individual now cycling up into hypomania (mania lite). In the bottom representation, we see bipolar I in action, with the cycle topping out at mania.

Today, the DSM recognizes the bottom two representations as being related, but not the top. Instead, the DSM would have us regard the top representation as part of plain vanilla unipolar depression.

If this makes no sense to you, you are in good company. The Swiss psychiatrist Jules Angst, you will recall, is one of two men who back in the sixties coined the term *unipolar* depression. But he is also extremely vocal in insisting that a good many of those diagnosed with unipolar simply don't belong there.

One of his arguments has to do with loosening the DSM criteria for hypomania. The DSM minimum time requirement is four days. But if we were to replace this with a two-day minimum, according to Dr Angst, we would double or triple the bipolar population, from about two percent to five or six percent.

Minor tweak, major result. The DSM-5 mood disorders work group actually seriously considered recommending the change, but (ironically due to a newer study Dr Angst was involved in) backed off. Instead, in the back, under "Conditions for Further Study," we have as a proposed diagnosis, "depressive episodes with short-duration hypomania."

More germane to our discussion is the fact that hypomania is virtually impossible to recognize in a clinical setting, especially when a patient walks in the door feeling depressed. In an ongoing study of nearly 6,000 patients published in the August 2011 *Archives of General Psychiatry*, Dr Angst found half these individuals were misdiagnosed with unipolar depression. A more thorough exam using sophisticated screening instruments could have avoided a lot of this.

In a 2013 editorial in the *International Journal of Bipolar Disorders*, Dr Angst reported that 40 percent of those diagnosed with major depression are "hidden bipolar."

Here is the problem: Try recalling how good you once felt while you are severely depressed. In this state, your brain is playing tricks on you. Memory fails you. Even raging manias—which are no-brainers to spot in real time and should be easy to recollect—fade into the dark shadows. Goodwin and Jamison, in *Manic-Depressive Illness*, cite a study that found that 60 percent of those showing up at their doctors depressed will deny ever having been admitted to the hospital for mania, even if the event is in their charts.

If the first psychiatrist I saw could have taken an x-ray of my life, he would have had no problem diagnosing me as bipolar I. The problem was that it never even occurred to me to tell him about how my over-the-top behavior made me unemployable twelve years earlier.

No, when something has taken over your brain—when all you can think about is throwing yourself off the balcony with a noose around your neck—you're not looking back at all your wacky wild times. Nor do you recall the simple joys in life— the birth of your child, the thrill of nailing a tough assignment, falling in love, what food tastes like, a spectacular sunset—none of it.

This leads us to our next consideration: "Is depression a matter of bipolar waiting to happen?"

In a study published in the February 2005 *Journal of Affective Disorders*, Dr Angst and his colleagues tracked 406 patients with major mood disorders over a 20-year period. Of 309 patients presenting with depression, four in ten eventually manifested as bipolar—one in four of these to bipolar I, and one in six to bipolar II. Throw in those who already had bipolar at the beginning of the study and those with bipolar at the end outnumbered those with depression.

The reason no one is jumping up and down screaming from the rooftops is because these changes were gradual— like global warming—at the rate of between .5 and one percent over 12 months. So in any given year, no one was likely to parse the results of a diagnostic head-count and go, holy crap!

But holy crap!

A single snapshot of an illness, in other words, should not be taken for the real thing. Even the DSM pays some regard to this, with its arbitrary days or weeks minimum requirements. But what about the long course? Could some unipolar depressions, in fact amount to one phase in the life-cycle of the same underlying condition?

Perhaps one day, a blood draw or brain scan or genetic read-out will give us a clear and authoritative picture of what is truly going on, and so spare patients and their families years of heartbreak and frustration. In the meantime, Drs Goodwin, Ghaemi, Akiskal, and numerous others are urging clinicians to ask more questions of their depressed patients—probe for age of first onset, family history, evidence of past depressions, failures on antidepressants, and more.

They are also asking us to consider the fact that unipolar and bipolar are hardly separate species, that there is in fact a vast herd of diagnostic rhinopotami grazing in plain sight along the bipolar spectrum. Call it what you want—bipolar III, highly recurrent depression, whatever. Just don't pretend it doesn't exist.

13. CONNECTING "UP" AND "DOWN"

Let's keep it simple, for now. Think of mania, hypomania, and depression in terms of "up" and "down." Two thousand years ago, Aretaeus of Cappadocia described both melancholia and mania and linked them to the same condition. Here is his partial description of "up":

Some patients with mania are cheerful, they laugh, play, dance day and night, they stroll in the market, sometimes with a garland on the head, as if they had been winner in a game: these patients do not bring worries to their relatives.

But "others fly into a rage."

As for melancholia:

The patients are dull or stern, dejected or unreasonably torpid, without any manifest cause ...

Aretaeus described fear and sleeplessness, and as the condition intensifies, patients "complain of life and desire to die."

Aretaeus also regarded mania as emerging from melancholia. Never mind for now whether this is actually the case. Let's simply acknowledge that by connecting the two—by pairing "up" to "down"—he became the first person we know of to identify what we would later call bipolar disorder. But to accomplish that, first he had to ask himself how two apparently opposite conditions could possibly be related.

This is completely contrary to the DSM polarity

mindset, which would have us believe that depression and mania exist independently of one another, that neither is influenced by the other. Cyclicity, on the other hand, asks us to think in terms of each state exerting a sort of gravitational pull on the other.

One simple way of approaching this, according to Dr Koukopoulos, is by viewing depression as the spent remains of mania or hypomania. In essence, our manic or hypomanic engine has run out. No gas in the tank, no power in the batteries. Or, as the Renaissance philosopher Marsilio Ficino put it: "The melancholic humor lights and burns, producing that excitement which the Greeks call mania and we furor. But when it dies out, only a black soot is left ..."

If you think this applies to you, then your best depression-prevention strategy may be an effective mania-prevention strategy. Mania and depression are connected. This is Dr Koukopoulos' point.

Map of reality close-up 2: Depression and mania aren't isolated events. Each exerts an effect on the other.

Dr Koukopoulos also points to studies that show when

patients are prematurely taken off lithium, they relapse initially into mania rather than depression, as if mania is the default pathology. In addition, we can make a very strong evolutionary biology case that depression is our body's way of telling us to slow down from our over-exertions—to rest, heal, reset all our biological systems.

But who has time for rest?

We can go a step further by pointing to winter depressions—most likely an artifact of a much earlier age —when our very survival depended on our ability to go into partial hibernation at certain times of the year. Unlike us, the ancients were very much aware of the most subtle changes in the seasons. As well as noticing the association between winter and melancholia, our ancestors couldn't help but observe that mania tends to break out in the summer.

Seasonal cycles. Cycles. Always cycles.

According to Dr Koukopoulos, moderns think of time as a linear progression rather than circular. One event follows the other, or may even have a timeless dimension, such as Freud's unconscious. With the ancients, by contrast, all of creation was in flux, but everything inevitably came back to the same place.

Dr Koukopoulos goes farther by tying in cyclicity to homeostasis. Homeostasis has to do with the zillion and one biological processes that maintain our equilibrium. The principle explains, for instance, why our blood pressure and body temperature and so on remain fairly constant. In a similar vein, our nervous system tends to push depression back toward normal and level off manic tendencies.

In our enthusiasm to treat episodes in isolation, however, we lose track of the fact that our meds interfere with homeostasis. We can view bipolar as a breakdown in homeostasis—the thermostat isn't working. At the same time, an ill-considered meds strategy may make a bad situation worse. Anti-manic meds may push us into a depressive stupor. Antidepressants may induce mania and speed up cycling.

As Oregon psychiatrist Jim Phelps stresses over and over again in his 2006 book, *Why Am I Still Depressed*, we need to treat the cycle rather than the symptom du jour.

Recall my Chernobyl experience in my car following a disastrous outing. A few weeks later, I rolled the dice on a cross-country trip to New York, with similarly horrific results. Had I stayed home on both occasions, my brain would have stayed quiet. But ships aren't designed to stay in harbors, nor cars in garages.

All this was at the top of my mind nine or ten months later when I was contemplating driving 2,400 miles up and back from San Diego to attend a didgeridoo gathering in Oregon. The word didgeridoo should red-flag the fact that I have not entirely grasped the concept of normal, and thank heaven for that.

Stay with me—you will see where this is going in a second.

In my perfect world, everyone would play the didgeridoo. Once a year, for one brief shining moment, that perfect world comes into existence—a Camelot, a Brigadoon village of didgeridoo people, my tribe coming together in a clearing in a forest.

I had been to two previous gatherings, but in the company of a girlfriend, who, in a pinch, could take over as my frontal lobes. This time, no girlfriend. I like to joke that I prefer driving with my eyes closed. Heaven help if I have to look.

Throw on top of that all the things that can go wrong on disrupted sleep with a brain that I should have returned to the customer service counter of life five minutes after I was born.

No. The prudent choice was to stay home.

But here's the thing. As the gathering drew closer, I felt myself sliding into a depression. The thought of not being with my tribe was too much for me to bear. Call it biology, call it a maladaptive response, I was not reacting at all well to this. Staying home was only going to make it worse.

The bipolar's dilemma: Take a chance and risk a meltdown? Play it safe and suffer the effects of social isolation? Up and down—they're connected.

Screw it. At the last minute, I found someone to travel with me part-way who was willing to drive. I stuffed my camping gear and three didgeridoos into the back of my car, and headed out the door at one in the morning. That's right, no sleep.

A few hours later, with no traffic to speak of, we were clear of LA. I let out a whoop of delight. I was on my way. Two days later, I was where I needed to be, waking up under the trees to the irresistible call of the didgeridoo. My heaven may be your hell. Just don't ask me to go on a smooth jazz cruise with you.

A blessed stillness coupled by enhanced awareness, an inner calm. A comfort within myself combined with a sense of connectedness. On the way home, I spent a couple of days in Sequoia National Park. I broke out my new didgeridoo and sounded a cosmic OM into the forest.

"Keep close to Nature's heart," said John Muir, "and break clear away, once in a while, and climb a mountain or spend a week in the woods. Wash your spirit clean."

Just what the doctor ordered.

14. THE BIPOLAR SPECTRUM AND MIXED STATES

Now that we're clear on how our cycling links depression and mania and normal, we will conceptualize the bipolar spectrum in a different but complementary way. Below is a photo I took with my iPhone.

Note the extreme contrasts, natural light and dark facing off, all hell about to break loose. Okay, now that you have the visual, I can explain "mixed states." As always, Kraepelin was onto it first. According to the old master:

Very often, we meet temporarily with states which do not exactly correspond to manic excitement or to depression, but represent a mixture of morbid symptoms ... This relationship becomes most clear in the transition periods from one state to another, which often extend over weeks or months.

Depression and mania cycling into each other.

Kraepelin adds another layer of sophistication to this by plotting our cycles in three alternating wave patterns of intellect, emotion, and volition. The diagram below is from his 1921 *Manic-Depressive Illness*. I have overlaid two darker squares. In the left-most square, we see the three waves occupying mania, but free-falling into depression. In the right square, two of the waves have dropped below the "normal" horizon into depression, while one remains above in mania. This represents a mixed state. Where the lines eventually converge at the bottom we have "pure" depression.

Then the pattern repeats in reverse on the cycles' upward course through mixed states and back into pure mania.

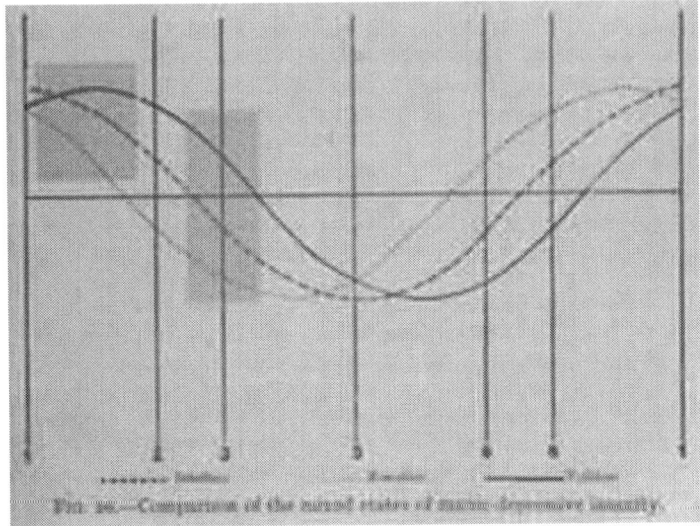

Fig. 94.—Comparison of the normal states of manic-depressive insanity.

This, Kraepelin explains, is why we may find ourselves in various states of animated despair or funky highs. The old master came up with six different categories of mixed states, which we can simplify (as do others) into agitated depressions and dysphoric manias. For right now, let's not bother trying to distinguish one from the other. Instead, simply recall that last time you experienced road rage, whether you were in a car or not. That sort of describes it.

Picture yourself, for instance, in Walmart, wanting to run down all the shoppers with your cart, just prior to bursting into tears by the 500-pound bags of dry dog food.

I once fired God. God and I have issues. There's a passage in Homer's *Iliad* that best gives expression to how I was feeling. This is when the Greeks' mighty warrior, Achilles, discovers that the god Apollo has played a trick on him (in my case, this involved God hiding my car keys just as I needed to head out the door for an important meeting). As Homer describes it: "Achilles of the nimble feet was furious."

I looked up at the ceiling. "God, you're fired!" I shouted.

So—this is what a mixed state sort of looks like. As it turned out, a few minutes later, God returned my keys, I settled down, and I got to my meeting on time, without incident. So, technically speaking, I was operating well within the range of "normal," or normal with hiccups.

But there have been times in my life where my Homeric sense of distress went on for days on end. "Rage! Goddess, sing the rage," reads the opening line to the *Iliad*. Tell me about it.

Kraepelin estimated the frequency of mixed states at 60 percent. More modern estimates (discarding the ones using ridiculously strict criteria) place it anywhere from the 20 to the 70 percent range. In other words, "mixed" may well be our most common mood presentation.

Not that you would know this by flicking through DSMs III through IV. Until the DSM-5 of 2013, a mixed state required the simultaneous presence of both full-blown depression and mania. This effectively made a rarity of mixed states. Introducing into the mix, say, "mixed depressive episode" (depression with some elements of mania) would have made a lie of "polarity." Imagine having to acknowledge that even "unipolar" depression could contain elements of "bipolar."

There goes your precious wall of diagnostic separation.

This is the point Dr Koukopoulos makes. Dr Koukopoulos virtually owns the term, "agitated depression." His argument—which I heard him expound on at length in Pittsburgh at the Fourth International Conference on Bipolar Disorder in 2001—is that unless the DSM expressly red-flags this variant, clinicians will continue to treat all depressions as the same.

Antidepressant down the hatch, in other words, which may only worsen the condition.

Now imagine the mix featuring mania or hypomania as the dominant presentation. Thus instead of experiencing "euphoric" highs, we enter a state of "dysphoric" distress, what Hagop Akiskal refers to as mania's "dark side." This might not look all that much different from agitated depression, but if you can get an accurate read on where you are now, you may be able to anticipate where your brain is going next.

As you are by now aware, our entire well-being depends on cultivating an ability to see over the bend in the horizon.

Dr Akiskal is the one most closely identified with the mood spectrum. Over the years, he has collaborated with an international team of researchers—most notably Olavo Pinto, Elie Hantouche, and the late Franco Benazzi—in teasing out in patient populations elements of mania in depression, and depression in mania. His bottom line is that these patients look very different from those presenting with pure depression or pure mania.

In addition, Dr Akiskal adds another twist to mixed states, one that builds on Kraepelin. As you recall, the old master viewed manic-depression as bleeding over into personality, and he devoted considerable time observing this in his patients. Thus, he noted, manic episodes were far more likely to arise from patients with "manic" temperaments than from those who were naturally down.

"State," in effect, emerges from "trait." In this context we can also view the mood spectrum in terms of our illness being an extension of our personalities.

Dr Akiskal took this a step farther by asking, in effect, what happens if opposite state meets opposite trait? Say someone who is naturally up who becomes depressed.

That depression, he argues, is going to look a lot different than someone who is naturally down to begin with. Can we call it a mixed state? Dr Akiskal does.

Once again, visualize me back in my car, with Chernobyl going off in my head. Galen the Physician, you will recall, was in front with me, contemplating my black and yellow bile, consulting with Emil Kraepelin, with Shakespeare helpfully suggesting "melancholic choler."

There you sort of have it, state meets trait.

By the time the DSM-5 Task Force set to work in 2006, the body of research evidence in favor of mixed states could not be explained away. In addition, at least two of the people on the DSM-5 mood disorders work group had published research articles on mixed states, including Ellen Frank of the University of Pittsburgh and Trisha Suppes of Stanford.

So it was—in one of the few things the DSM-5 did right—we find for the first time, on the unipolar side, "depressive disorder with mixed features" (unipolar depression with at least three hypomanic symptoms). Over on the bipolar end, we get, again for the first time, "manic or hypomanic episode with mixed features" (mania or hypomania with at least three depression symptoms), and "depressive episode with mixed features" (depression with at least three manic/hypomanic symptoms).

We can quibble over why the DSM-5 set the criteria at three symptoms rather than two, but the reality is that any clinician who takes stock in counting symptoms is not paying attention to his actual patient. It would have been far more helpful, instead, had the DSM-5 dispensed with the symptom-count entirely and actually told us what we were looking at—agitated depressions and dysphoric manias and hypomanias.

Map of reality close-ups 3 and 4: One way of conceptualizing mixed states is to imagine two trains speeding in opposite directions along the same set of tracks. In the top representation the trains meet up in depression, which may account for agitated depressions. In the bottom, the trains collide in mania (you can also imagine the impact occurring in hypomania), which would explain dysphoric manias and hypomanias.

Okay, what about anomalous symptoms, such as a patient laughing while describing her misery? At a session titled "Mixed Features in Depressive Episodes" at the 2015 US Psychiatric and Mental Health Congress in San Diego, I heard a panel of bipolar experts advise the clinicians in the audience to pay attention to such inconsistencies. But what do you call it? What does it signify? Who knows? We're only just starting to learn.

One final point: Clinicians and researchers frame their discussions in terms of threshold episodes. The reality, though, is we spend a good deal of our time, probably most of it, at the subthreshold level, below the diagnostic radar. Even in "normal," our psyches are constantly buffeted by the fluctuations of our moods and thoughts and energy levels, typically on mixed collision courses. These disturbances may not merit a clinician's attention, but far too often they are enough to ruin our day—day after day.

To freely interpret: Even our "normals" can be mixed.

Such is the nature of our cycles, nothing ever standing still, everything in motion. Cycling may well be the elegant and simple explanation for what takes place on the bipolar spectrum, but our mixed states serve as a sobering reminder of what tends to happen when simplicity, with the help of a trickster god or two, builds on itself.

Life suddenly becomes complicated.

Map of reality close-up 5: It is a mistake to think of "normal" as the absence of symptoms or as a refuge from the storm. In the depiction above, zooming in on normal reveals the dynamics of our map of reality playing out on a micro level.

15. KINDLING AND NEUROPLASTICITY, PLUS RAPID-CYCLING AND CYCLOTHYMIA

Does our bipolar worsen over time? For instance, if you zap lab animals in the amygdala—the part of the brain that kicks off fight or flight—the repeated exposure "kindles" the brain into spontaneous seizures. This is reasoning by analogy, but the inference is clear: That first episode has changed the brain in a way that increases our risk for a second episode. As Robert Post, principal exponent of the kindling hypothesis, puts it: "Episodes beget episodes."

Kraepelin, himself, observed that intervals between episodes grew shorter over time. He also noted that stress was less of a factor in triggering later episodes. The implication is that although life events may play a major role in initiating that first episode, after that the illness tends to take on a life of its own. Subsequent studies lend support to Kraepelin's findings.

In his 2008 book, *Treatment of Bipolar Illness*, Dr Post points to brain research that suggests the loss in the brain's ability to protect itself against successive episode outbreaks. As he concludes: "We always knew that affective episodes are associated with enormous suffering, but now they are likely to be bad for the brain."

Perhaps now you can understand why our doctors insist that we stay on our meds for years and years, if not for the rest of our lives. Goodwin and Jamison's look at the data, though, indicates that kindling may not be as universal as its proponents make it out to be. Nevertheless, it would be foolish to tempt fate.

But no discussion of kindling would be complete without raising two counter-arguments. The first concerns "successful aging." This term did not enter the medical literature until 1987. According to Colin Depp of UCSD, in a 2013 talk to the International Bipolar Foundation in San Diego, "This is the generation people have an opportunity to age well."

Studies conducted on the general population show that as people get older they tend to acquire an enviable set of coping skills and smart lifestyle practices that promote resilience and good health. In the long run, these may have a more protective effect than our meds.

To freely interpret, over time, we actually find ourselves enlisting the brain in our own recovery. This raises our second counter-argument, which involves "neuroplasticity." This has to do with the brain continually building newer versions of itself. Basically, "what fires together, wires together."

According to neuroplasticity pioneer Michael Merzenich of UCSF, we can be active agents in increasing or decreasing our neural signaling. These produce long-term structural changes that set us up for more positive behavioral outcomes.

How mind-boggling can this be? In one set of studies, Sarah Lazar of Harvard found that mindfulness meditation can actually decrease the size of the amygdala, involved in fight or flight, and increase cortical thickness. We have known for a long time that meditation and yoga and the like induce good feelings, but the effect was believed to be temporary, a sort of hormonally induced high.

Apparently, not so.

Thus a picture emerges of two contrasting forces at work, but they are most likely flip sides of the same phenomenon. On one side, the follies of youth and the stresses of middle age set us up for kindling and deterioration. On the other, the wisdom of old age encourages neuroplasticity and healing. The trick to recovery, then, could be to get smart at a much earlier stage in life.

But recovery is the last thing on your mind if you are experiencing your second major depression in a row or you are reeling from the disorienting whiplash from mania or hypomania to depression and back again in a matter of days. The phenomenon is "rapid-cycling," which can be viewed as one outcome of kindling.

The DSM mandates a minimum of four episodes a year, spaced out by periods of remission. But a good many patients can go from up to down and back again within days. Technically, they have failed to meet the time minimum (two weeks for depression, seven days for mania, four days for hypomania) for an episode. The DSM gets around this problem by failing to acknowledge the situation.

Real-world psychiatry, nevertheless, recognizes those who experience "ultra-rapid" and "ultradian" cycling. Try to imagine the terror of lurching from one emotional extreme to another in the space of days or even hours.

Or, if your rapid-cycling proceeds at more of a DSM pace, try to imagine that sense of relief you experienced after emerging from a crushing three-month depression. Then, say, a month later, your luck runs out. The bottom falls out of you. Here we go again.

For a condition capable of so much distress, we know very little about it. A 2014 literature search conducted by a team of leading international researchers came up with just 119 relevant articles. In a review article they published in the June 2014 *Journal of Clinical Psychiatry*, among other things, the authors observed:

- Many more women than men experience rapid-cycling.
- The condition is fairly common, but not necessarily permanent.
- It is associated with a younger age of bipolar onset.
- Suicidality and alcohol and drug abuse are more common among those who rapid-cycle.
- There is an overlap with mixed states.
- There is a possible association with hypothyroidism.
- Antidepressant treatment may set off rapid-cycling, but further study evidence is needed.
- The prevailing view is that the condition is more associated with bipolar II, but other studies suggest a stronger association with bipolar I.

If you are one of those who experience rapid-cycling, keep in mind that your immediate goal is to achieve stability, or at least learn to anticipate and adapt. A lot of people with bipolar—rapid-cycler or not—don't seem to get going until well into the day. Then, in the evening, they may experience an energy surge that keeps them fully engaged well into the evening and makes going to sleep at a normal time highly problematic. There are no easy solutions, but being able to spot these and other patterns at least lets you know what you're dealing with.

Closely related to rapid-cycling is cyclothymia. Recall from Chapter Six where Kraepelin characterized some of his patients as "cyclothymic." These were people who experienced mild ups and downs as a natural part of their personality. Hagop Akiskal also uses the term in this fashion.

The DSM, however, views cyclothymia as an illness, a form of bipolar lite. These patients experience a chronic condition of fluctuating mood disturbances without breaking into full-blown episodes. The cumulative effect, though, is likely to cause great personal distress and interfere with normal functioning.

There is no right or wrong interpretation of cyclothymia, here. At this level, where illness bleeds into personality, it is virtually impossible to separate the two. In later chapters, we will explore this issue with regard to hypomania (mania lite) and dysthymia (low grade chronic depression). For right now, however, let's simply acknowledge the cycling presence and the effect that even its slightest expressions may have on our overall well-being.

16. FIGURING OUT OUR ILLUSION

Said Einstein: "Reality is merely an illusion, albeit a very persistent one." I would suggest that we find ourselves with the opportunity to pierce through the illusion when, out of nowhere, we find reality opportunistically asserting itself, inevitably with devastating effect. As much as we might like to live in another reality, our illness forces us to come to terms with this one. "Know thyself" takes on a new urgency.

Maybe one day a new reality will present itself. Maybe one day, in effect, we can trade illusions. But for that to happen, first we need to figure out this one.

This wraps up Part II. To summarize:

We looked at bipolar's close relation to recurrent depression, which forces us to consider the two as occupying an overlapping and continuous spectrum.

In addition, we looked at how depression and mania do not exist in isolation, how each exerts a gravitational pull on the other. Awareness of this can make a huge difference in managing our cycles.

We also examined the spectrum in terms of "mixed" states, where depression meets mania in the form of agitated depressions and dysphoric manias. An easy way to look at this is to think of road rage, even if you're not driving.

We also looked at the issue of kindling and how episodes may beget episodes. Rapid-cycling may be an expression of this. Running counter to this is the notion of successful aging and neuroplasticity.

We also need to appreciate that even if we do successfully manage our illness, we face daily challenges.

Even in "normal," we are buffeted by our moods and anxieties and energy levels, not to mention dictated to by the bonds of our temperaments and the caprices of our environment. Thus, even under-the-radar symptoms of short duration may be enough to cause great personal distress.

Let's keep exploring ...

PART THREE: MAPPING UP

O love, be moderate, allay thy ecstasy,
  In measure rain thy joy, scant this excess!

  —Shakespeare, A Midsummer Night's Dream

17. HOW HIGH IS "UP"?

In this field, no one has the answers. Even if we ask the right questions, each answer is bound to yield a hundred more questions. But ask we must. So let's start with this deceptively simple query: How high is up?

Kraepelin's 1921 *Manic-Depressive Insanity* notes "the slightest forms of manic excitement are usually called hypomania." The patients he observed tended to be lively and not at all disordered, though he did detect a certain "lack of an inner unity in the course of ideas."

The DSM-III of 1980 left hypomania out of its symptom list line-up, but in its descriptive narrative for mania noted that "hypomania is similar to, but not as severe as ... mania."

The DSM-III-R of 1987 added to and refined its severity criteria, which, with a minor word change or two, has remained constant into the present. Thus, for mania:

The mood disturbance is sufficiently severe to cause marked impairment in occupational functioning or in usual social activities or relationships with others ...

And for hypomania:

The disturbance is NOT [emphasis mine] severe enough to cause marked impairment in social or occupational functioning or to require hospitalization ...

In other words, hypomania—whether euphoric or dysphoric—is not a pathology in and of itself. Your wheels may be spinning entirely too fast for your own comfort,

95

but for right now the train is still on the tracks, the engineer is still at the controls. If disaster does occur—ruined credit, a wrecked relationship—it is within the context of functioning within an amped up version of "normal."

David Dunner of the University of Washington first proposed bipolar II—recurrent depression interspersed with hypomania—back in the early 1970s. In 1976, he co-authored an article that noted the clinical course and family histories in this population could be distinguished from bipolar I (bipolar with mania) and unipolar depression.

Dr Dunner's version of bipolar II was formally incorporated into the DSM-IV of 1994. The significance of the diagnosis is the acknowledgement that the "up" in question tops out at hypomania, with no escalation into mania. Kraepelin, though he recognized hypomania, never thought to subdivide manic-depression in this fashion.

You can say that Kraepelin's view of manic-depression would have embraced bipolar II. It's just that carving manic-depression into several pieces violated his own principle of unity.

This historical context is vital to our understanding of bipolar II. There has been no end of popular commentary —nearly all of it uninformed—suggesting that bipolar II is a fad diagnosis or a "soft" version of bipolar. This only makes sense if you view the bipolar II version of "up" in isolation, as if we were looking at a harmless school of pilot fish unaccompanied by that great white shark of a depression.

Sorting out hypomania from any "normal" upbeat mood is difficult enough to accomplish in real time, never mind trying to recall the last time you felt good while submerged beneath a crushing depression. No one has ever visited a psychiatrist for the first time complaining about being in a wonderful mood. Virtually all of us show up severely depressed, and this poses a major problem.

According to one study, psychiatrists initially misdiagnose half of us. If a primary care physician is conducting the exam, the rate of misdiagnosis shoots up to eight in ten.

According to another study, eight to 10 years elapse from time of first onset to a correct diagnosis. According to two DBSA surveys from 1994 and 2000, one-third of those misdiagnosed remain that way for a decade. Typically, these patients are subjected to endless rounds of antidepressants that are likely to make their condition worse, even much worse, not better.

Major alert: antidepressants and bipolar do not mix.

We will get into this in a later chapter, and into considerable detail in a future book. What we need to appreciate for right now is that misdiagnosis leaves us highly vulnerable. As well as being exposed to medication with a considerable risk of causing us great harm, somewhere between a quarter and a half of us will attempt suicide at least once. Left untreated (or mistreated), fifteen percent of us will succumb. Among bipolar I and bipolar II, guess which population is most likely to be left out in the cold? Fad diagnosis? Don't get me started.

So maybe we're better off ripping up the symptom lists and acknowledging that "up" only has to be higher than "down." Never mind distinguishing hypomania from normal. We are simply looking for a history of lucid intervals between depressions. But in order to do that, first we need to find evidence of those past depressions. These should be a lot easier to recall than those times you felt way too good for your own good, or even just okay.

"Have you ever felt this miserable before?"

Easiest question in the world to answer, but trust me, your family doctor won't bother asking it. A psychiatrist worth her salt will make the query and ask follow-up questions, make prompts.

"Did your grades ever slip in high school?"

Remember? Way back? That's right. The time you went from an honors student to barely passing. Was it depression? Maybe. Slowly a history builds, one of recurring depressions. Perhaps they are lining up like pointer stars to that bear of a constellation representing bipolar.

Perhaps now, your psychiatrist feels sufficiently confident to probe for evidence of when you may have felt better than normal. Dr Akiskal, with tongue in cheek, talks of the "rule of three," such as proficiency in three or more languages (rare in the US), having worked in three fields that require personal charm and eloquence (such as diplomacy, journalism, and entertainment), excelling in three or more creative domains, attending three universities without getting a degree, and so on.

In all seriousness, though, these are the kinds of patterns an alert clinician can pick up in a patient who only wants to talk about how miserable she has been all her life.

Let's briefly bring Dr Goodwin into the picture. He is adamant that a family member needs to be in on the consultation. If you fail, for instance, to recall the time you loudly demanded a fine Chablis in a redneck dive in Bakersfield your loved one certainly will.

This bears emphasis and re-emphasis: Once we are engulfed in depression, it's as if our good times—all of them—have been wiped from our memory banks. Our psychiatrists are only as good as what we tell them.

Unfortunately, we have become our own least reliable narrators.

Two mania/hypomania screening tools act as clinical prompts. These include the 13-item Mood Disorders Questionnaire (MDQ) and the 32-item Hypomania/Mania Checklist (HCL-32). Both, for instance, ask about feeling more talkative than usual and racing thoughts and needing less sleep and so on. The HCL-32 gets into more detail by inquiring into such things as colorful clothes and make-up and making more puns and jokes when talking.

But the major red flag item for both the MDQ and HCL-32 is having more energy and (for the HCL-32) engaging in more activity than usual. According to Dr Angst, in the 2011 study cited in Chapter Twelve, half and three-quarters of bipolar patients respectively responded positively to this item.

It's almost as if we could scrap the other questions altogether and just zero in on the energy/overactivity factor. Significantly, the DSM-5 added "increased energy or activity" to "elevated, expansive, or irritable mood" as its criteria for mania and hypomania.

Dr Angst found in his study that the use of these screening instruments did pick up an impressive number of patients who would ordinarily have been diagnosed with unipolar depression. But this gets us back to our initial question: How high is up?

In other words, why set the bar so high at hypomania in the first place? Just so there are no misunderstandings: Recognizing "up" and managing "up" are two entirely different considerations. The first is a diagnostic issue, the second a treatment/recovery issue. But if we fail to recognize "up" in the first place, treatment and recovery become nonstarters.

This is much the point Dr Phelps makes on his website,

PsychEducation. According to Dr Phelps, in looking for evidence of hypomania in a patient's history, we are essentially asking the wrong question, namely: Do you HAVE bipolar? Rather, the proper question should be: How MUCH bipolar do you have?

Dr Phelps points to Harvard University's Bipolarity Index, developed by Gary Sachs. There, actual symptoms account for only one-fifth of the total picture.

Again, keep in mind that when you are depressed, recalling when you felt good is next to impossible. Doctors need other things to go on, including, according to the Bipolarity Index:

- Age of onset of first mood symptoms (bipolar tends to manifest in one's teens or early adulthood).
- Illness course and other features generally only visible over time (such as recurrent depressions).
- Response to medications (such as bad reactions to antidepressants or favorably responding to bipolar meds).
- Family history of mood and substance problems (such as a first or second degree relative with bipolar).

Drumroll ...

Here's the crazy part. The DSM-5 actually includes as a category of bipolar "Other Specified Bipolar and Related Disorders." This is an update of the DSM-IV's "Bipolar Disorder Not Otherwise Specified" (NOS). The DSM-IV mentions that NOS includes bipolar features that do not meet specific bipolar criteria.

The DSM-5 further elaborates by noting these features may include hypomanias "with insufficient symptoms."

It's all there in the fine print, but who reads the fine print?

In 2011, the World Health Organization published a study showing the lifetime prevalence of bipolar worldwide. For bipolar I it was 0.6 percent, and 0.4 percent for bipolar II. "Subthreshold bipolar"—essentially what the DSM files under NOS but which gets misdiagnosed as unipolar depression—is 1.4. "Bipolar spectrum disorder"—think of those who cycle in and out of highly recurrent depression—is 2.6 percent. Five percent of the population in all.

In the US, the figures are considerably higher: Bipolar I —1.0 percent, bipolar II—1.1 percent, subthreshold—2.4, bipolar spectrum—4.4. Nearly nine percent of the population in all.

Again, why don't we simply acknowledge that "up" only needs to be higher than "down"?

Map of reality close-up 6: Distinguishing "normal" from hypomania. Note how mania stops at bipolar I, represented by the red line to the right and hypomania stops at the middle red line signifying bipolar II. But reconceptualizing "up" as simply higher than down

would incorporate "normal" into our mood states and force us to pay attention to recurrent depression on the left.

18. IS "UP" YOUR TRUE NORMAL?

In the previous chapter, we asked: How high is "up"? This leads us to our next question: Is "up" your true normal? Consider the following ...

Two women are dancing on tables. It's not the dancing on tables that is at issue—it's who is dancing on tables. One is Marilyn Monroe. The other is your stereotypical librarian. Marilyn is obviously just being Marilyn. It's the librarian we need to worry about. Then again, she may be fine.

"I hate to tell you this," a good friend of mine told me. "You're normal."

The bottom dropped out of me. Normal? Normal is a word you only want to hear after you've had a colonoscopy. My mother once sat me down on her knee and said, "Son, there's no excuse for dancing like a white man." Okay, I'm making that up, but seriously, who wants to be normal?

No insult to this fine group of individuals, mind you. Some of my best friends are normal. Wait—what the hell am I talking about?—no they're not. These people bore the crap out of me. Screw them, I avoid them like the plague. I mean, has anyone ever said to you: "You're in for a special treat. We're going to meet some incredibly normal people."

But that's not what my friend meant by normal. Kay Jamison's 2004 book *Exuberance* offers some insight. "We have given sorrow many words," she writes, "but passion for life few." Exuberance, she says, "takes us many places," with "delight its own reward, adventure its own pleasure."

These are people who tend to see their work as play. "I

103

can't understand why they pay me to do what I love," Robert Farquhar of the Johns Hopkins Applied Physics Laboratory told Dr Jamison. In 2001, he and his team successfully landed a spacecraft on the asteroid Eros. His enthusiasm, he said, gave him the staying power to persevere over the NASA bureaucrats, who would have been satisfied with a mere orbital mission.

Dr Jamison also mentions the author Virginia Woolf, best remembered for her madness and suicide, who tends to be forgotten as the person who lit up London's Bloomsbury Group. Said a colleague: "I always felt on leaving her that I had drunk two excellent glasses of champagne. She was a life-enhancer."

As much as society benefits from exuberant people, though, the world is also wary of them. As Dr Jamison points out: In *The House at Pooh Corner*, Rabbit and his cronies conspire to give the "too bouncy" Tigger a personality makeover and turn him into "a different Tigger altogether ... a Humble Tigger ... a sad Tigger, a Melancholy Tigger, a Small and Sorry Tigger."

Happily, the plan backfires, but that is not often the way things turn out in real life. Perhaps we can interpret this as a call to arms. Most of us know Dr Jamison as the author of *An Unquiet Mind*, which recounts her own struggles with mania and depression. But in *Exuberance*, she opens up to the joyous side of normal.

So where is our true normal?

Map of reality close-up 7: The three red lines representing bipolar I, bipolar II, and recurrent depression are anchored in our personalities and temperaments. Any judgment regarding "normal" or not needs to pay regard to personality.

Teddy Roosevelt was Dr Jamison's exuberant poster boy. According to a Harvard classmate, "he zoomed, he boomed, he bolted wildly." A journalist said that after you went home from a meeting with him you had to "wring the personality out of your clothes."

In her book, Dr Jamison focuses on TR's association with fellow exuberant, the naturalist John Muir, which set the stage for his legacy as a conservationist. But we can also make an argument that TR was an accident waiting to happen. Woodrow Wilson characterized him as "the most dangerous man of the age," and Mark Twain described him as "clearly insane."

This was a man whose unbounded enthusiasm led the US into one high-stakes imperialist venture after another. Fortunately, he never met his Vietnam.

Fast-forward to the end of 1967 and *Time* magazine's Man of the Year cover, with Lyndon Johnson caricatured as Lear. "A sovereign shame so elbows him," said Kent in the play. "These things sting His mind so venomously."

LBJ had met his Vietnam. Like TR, he was constantly "up" and enjoyed a lifetime of one success after another.

Probably no President accomplished more to greater lasting effect in his first three years in office than he had. Then in 1965 he decided to massively increase troop levels in what looked like a low-risk foreign intervention.

The decision was a rational one, made in consultation with his advisers. But by 1966, it was clear his position was untenable. In her 1976 book, *Lyndon Johnson and the American Dream*, historian Doris Kearns Goodwin recounts his unraveling:

> *In the past, Johnson had displayed a fine sense of discrimination about his political opponents, recognizing his enemies today might be his allies tomorrow. Now he became unrestrained and reckless, creating a fantasy world of heroes and villains. Members of the White House staff who had listened to the violent name-calling were frightened by what seemed to them signs of paranoia.*

Three months following the Lear cover—virtually unable to govern and with his popular support eroding by the day—Johnson announced that "I will not seek, nor will I accept, the nomination of my party for another term as your President."

He left office at the beginning of 1969, never to return to public life. He died four years later, an embittered and broken man.

Both TR and LBJ would easily meet the DSM criteria for hypomania. Just start with symptom number one —"inflated self-esteem or grandiosity"—and work your way down through "decreased need for sleep" and "more talkative than usual" and so on to "excessive involvement in activities that have a high potential for painful consequences."

From there, it is tempting to go through their lives to find a period where they may have experienced depression (TR certainly did), then retrospectively diagnose both of them with bipolar. But as tempting as it would be to claim two ex-presidents as members of our club, the truth is they were far too busy leading successful lives over an unbroken succession of decades for them to ever consider finding common cause with us.

Trust me, you won't find people with TR or LBJ qualities in bipolar support groups.

No, the real bipolar lesson is far more elemental and profound—we're "normal." It's just that in our particular versions of normal, our thoughts and feelings run a lot wider and deeper. Once we're on board with this, we are free from the tyranny of symptom lists and all those who point fingers in our direction. But we also need to acknowledge that wider and deeper is not always a blessing. In this sense, we're all accidents waiting to happen.

Dr Jamison used the term exuberance. Hagop Akiskal refers to "hyperthymic." Hyperthymic is the "trait," hypomania the "state." On the surface, the two appear exactly the same, but the first represents one person's "normal," the second another person's not-so-normal.

Recall Marilyn and the librarian dancing on tables. Marilyn is the "normal" one in the room.

But, as Dr Akiskal notes, taking his lead from Kraepelin, hypomanic and manic states may arise out of hyperthymic traits. This may have happened to Marilyn when her life unraveled at the very end.

A good doctor, of course, will work with you in finding your way to your true normal. The catch is your doctor's version of normal is likely to be very different from your own version, especially if her first impression was when she observed you bouncing off of walls and ceilings in a hospital ward.

According to John Gartner, associate professor at Johns Hopkins and author of the 2004 book, *The Hypomanic Edge*, writing in a July 2011 blog piece on *Psychology Today*, most patients with bipolar II regard their hypomania—what Dr Akiskal refers to as hyperthymia—as part of their temperament. They were born that way and have lived that way since they can remember. Writes Dr Gartner:

It is the source of their energy, creativity, productivity and identity. All they want is to be a better adjusted version of themselves. Trying to turn them into people of normal temperament is about as sensible and humane as trying to make a gay patient straight.

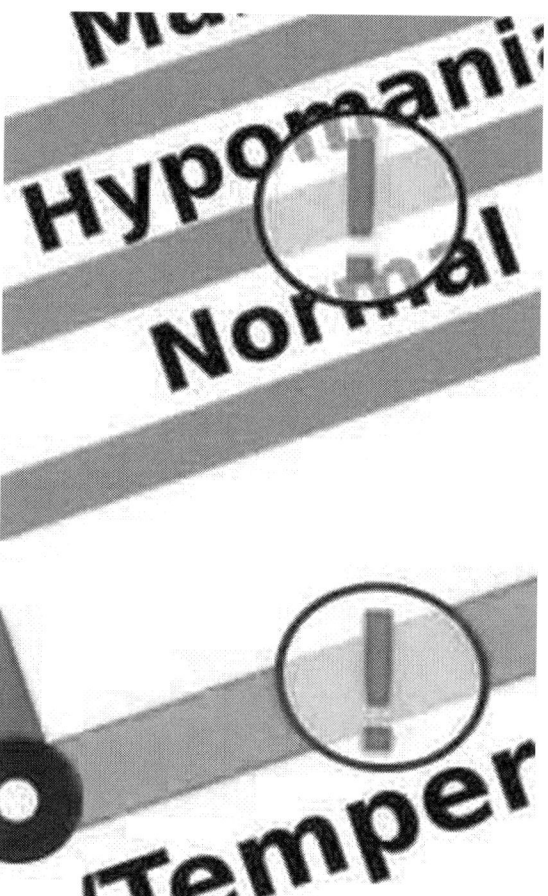

Map of reality, close-up 8: Same behavior, different context. The bottom exclamation point represents "exuberance," which is associated with the personality/temperament trait of "hyperthymia." With some people, behavior such as dancing on tables may be considered within the individual's "normal." The individual is in control and well inside her comfort zone, free to consider the risk/ benefits of her actions.

In someone else, the exact same behavior may point to "hypomania." The individual's behavior is not necessarily alarming, but it is clearly out of character. The individual is not totally in control and is venturing outside of her comfort zone, not in the best shape to consider the consequences of her actions.

But your doctor doesn't trust "up," and neither does society. This, I submit, accounts for most treatment failures in bipolar. A 2003 study co-authored by Jan Scott of Newcastle University found a major disconnect between doctors and their patients. The psychiatrists in the study thought that bipolar patients went off their meds because we "miss our highs." The patients who quit cited other reasons.

You can imagine how this went over at my first and last grand rounds ever in Princeton, New Jersey.

So here I was, with the Scott study up on my PowerPoint, and my audience responding as if to the opening scene in "Springtime for Hitler." It didn't help when the next thing out of my mouth was: "Get over it. When your patients complain to you about feeling like fat stupid zombie eunuchs on the meds you prescribe—and on the meds you overprescribe—they are not doing this to ruin your day."

To this day, I have no idea why they headed for the exits the second my lips stopped moving.

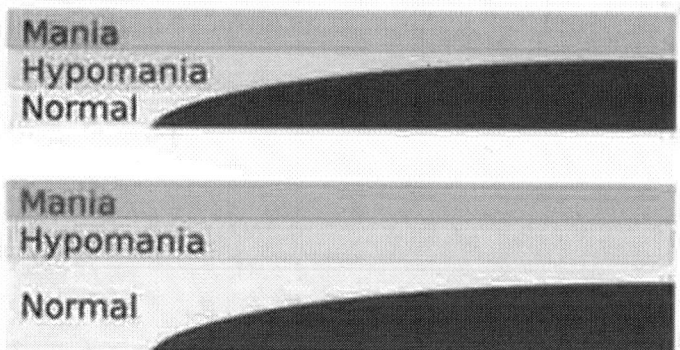

Marilyn vs the librarian. "Up" is relative. The top diagram above represents a classic case of our hypothetical librarian cycling into the uncomfortable high end of hypomania, close to losing control, just below the manic threshold. On the bottom diagram representing Marilyn, the cycling image is exactly the same. But check out the wider bandwidth. Her version of "normal" allows her a lot more clearance.

19. WHEN "UP" GOES WRONG, PART I: BIPOLAR II, HYPOMANIA, AND ANXIETY

Perhaps something like this has happened to you …

Blogger Willa Goodfellow, who describes herself as "good at parties," with good social skills, recounts being invited to tag along with her wife at a function at the home of Sally Mason, president of the University of Iowa.

Anticipating wine at the function, she decided to skip her afternoon Valium. Besides, she wanted to be mentally sharp. Later into the function, the host engaged the two in a conversation. They were standing in front of a bookcase populated with books by Iowa Writers Workshop authors. The workshop is the pride and joy of the university.

In Willa's words, "That is when the evil twin appeared." Pointing to a Pulitzer book, *Gilead* by Marilynne Robinson, the evil twin let loose: "Boring. Boring, boring, boring."

Gracious host that she was, Dr Mason acknowledged it was a difficult book to read. Willa says she could have redeemed herself by offering that it was difficult for her, as well. But, no. Willa pointed to another book. As she reports: "This time I said, 'I hate this book ...'" Dr Mason moved on to other guests.

I first encountered Willa's blog, *Prozac Monologues*, in 2009, when she was a few months into it. One quick sample:

For the Israelites, the Babylonian Exile resulted in an explosion of creativity, poetry, philosophy, history, new forms of worship, the legal code, and the development of a religion that was larger than their

prior notions of land=success=God's favor. They came up with a
religion that could handle exile, handle loss. It could travel and face
the future.

Their brains found new patterns. ...

In no time, we were exchanging emails. Willa is in her
fifties, an ordained Episcopalian priest who has the whole
God to neurons territory covered. A sampling from the
neurons side:

I'm into changing my brain. In that mass of electrical wiring,
some potentially healthy pathways are blocked by the detritus of dead
dendrites. Other destructive pathways are carved into canyons of well-
worn automatic responses.

Changing my brain will take time. It is taking decades. It will
take at least another blogpost.

Willa now lives in central Oregon with her wife, Helen.
She has a grown son from a previous marriage. In 2012,
we had the chance to meet face-to-face. The occasion was
the NAMI (National Alliance for the Mentally Ill) annual
convention in Chicago. It was the opening night dinner. I
was seated at a table with some of the people from our
local San Diego affiliate.

Willa popped over and said hi. My face lit up in
recognition. I pulled up a chair for her, and instantly we
hit it off—God, neurons, everything. Soon, a Latin band
started up and we were on the dance floor, along with half
our table. Two days later, we were seated over breakfast
sandwiches, once again talking about everything under
the sun.

Clearly Willa is one of those people who light up those
around her. But she also experiences depression, not to
mention occasional unwanted visits from that evil twin of

hers.

Willa, outside the St James Gate of the Guinness Brewery in Dublin. (Photo by Helen Keefe.)

We associate hypomania with that mysterious essence we wish we could put in a bottle and sell. In the popular mind, this is the kind of makeover we all pray will happen to us—salesperson of the month productivity combined with life-of-party sociability, with a bit of God and three of your favorite humans thrown in.

Who wouldn't want to be like this forever? But—alas!—

the sun rises, the sun sets. The wind blows to the south and turns to the north. Hypomania may start off as Gene Kelly singing in the rain, but next thing we may be experiencing the sensation of Laurel and Hardy chasing a piano down the stairs.

You are fine, mind you. Nothing wrong with you. But on some quantum level, without your knowledge, someone has picked up the entire universe and set it back down in not quite the right place. We may be off by only the width of a single Higgs Boson, but that's enough to throw your interface with social reality entirely off.

For some strange reason, people look at you funny. Your brilliant bon mots sail right over their heads, they don't laugh at your jokes, they affect to ignore you. Maybe they didn't get it right the first time, you decide. So you repeat yourself. You talk louder, like a tourist to a shop assistant who only speaks Hungarian.

This may have been what Kraepelin was referring to when he described a certain "lack of an inner unity in the course of ideas."

Now people are talking over you. Idiots! Don't they have any manners? Did someone just walk away from me? Someone is tugging on your sleeve. It's your partner. She's looking upset. Now what? you wonder.

If we're lucky, our hypomania tops out right here, while we are mere walking-talking social disasters. At least no one is throwing a net over our head or dialing 911. After all, this is a state that on its own doesn't warrant consideration as a pathology. How worse can things possibly get?

Funny you should ask. While working on the American Psychiatric Association's 2000 DSM IV-TR (a technical update), Trisha Suppes of Stanford University had an epiphany. "I said, wait," she told a UCLA grand rounds webcast in April 2003, "where are all those patients of mine who are hypomanic and say they don't feel good?"

Think of the opposite of Kay Jamison's exuberance. Dr Suppes uses road rage as a metaphor. Why was there no mention of that in hypomania? she wondered. A subsequent literature search yielded virtually no data.

These, of course, are the mixed states—in this context dysphoric hypomania—we referred to in Chapter Ten. This is where you fire God and run over people with your shopping cart. In a study published in 2005, Dr Suppes tracked 908 patients over seven years. Of those recognized as having hypomania, nearly 60 percent fit her criteria for dysphoric hypomania.

That's a lot of unhappy people ruining a lot of other people's days. Thanks to Dr Suppes and others, in 2013 the DSM finally recognized this dirty dark secret of "up." That's right—much of the time hypomania actually sucks. But, looking on the bright side, how much worse can things get, right?

You had to ask. For the first time—actually a century after Kraepelin—the DSM added to hypomania this specifier: "With anxious distress." This same specifier also appears with mania and depression.

You know the feeling. You're keyed up, on edge, burdened by worry, barely holding it together. Imagine yourself outside your car with a ticking nuclear bomb in the trunk with your keys locked inside—that sort of describes it.

The likely connecting link is stress. Think of the amygdala—that tiny part of the brain which kicks off fight or flight—launching a plate of spaghetti against the wall. In this context, some of what sticks is mania/hypomania, some of it anxiety. Once again, keep in mind that our brains are not organized according to DSM categories.

Hagop Akiskal sees anxiety occupying the same spectrum as depression and mania, from temperament (think of people with "nervous" dispositions) to illness. He is supported by a ton of his own and other people's research, plus no end of population studies. The most definitive one, part of the National Comorbidity Survey Replication from 2007 in which he took part, reveals that three in every four individuals with bipolar also experience a form of full-blown anxiety.

The numbers make a compelling case that we need to think of anxiety as a core bipolar feature, one that merits the same status and respect as depression and hypomania and mania. Conventional psychiatry views anxiety as a separate group of disorders that may be "comorbid" (ie co-occurring) with bipolar.

For our own well-being, though, we need to keep in mind that our neural circuits don't necessarily make these distinctions, and that when our minds start running away from us a lot of things are going on, sometimes at once, sometimes in sequences.

In addition, unlike conventional psychiatry, our brains don't simply dismiss less severe forms of anxiety. All of us experience a little bit of anxiety, and just this little bit (the technical term is "subsyndromal") is enough to massively complicate the course of our illness—in effect turn our "pure" states into mixed ones and perhaps kickstart our mood episodes.

Map of reality close-ups 9 and 10: Anxiety is typically viewed as an outgrowth of stress, part of the complex interactions between our genes and the environment, as depicted above. But the high prevalence of anxiety in bipolar also demands that we think of the condition as a core feature of our illness, along with depression and mania and hypomania.

Map of reality close-up 11: We also need to have regard for the fact that anxiety can mix with other mood states, as depicted below. Here, the trains collide in hypomania. Just as easily, the collision may occur in depression and mania.

The DSM-5 lists a number of different types of anxiety —including generalized, social, phobias, and panic—but let's not worry about diagnostic fine points. Basically, our irrational fears and worries have a way of kicking off panic or a sense of helplessness. Typically, we cope by adopting "avoidant" and other socially unuseful behaviors.

So, let's say you have a fear of driving that leads you to not renew your license. Decades pass. Suddenly, you realize you need to get back behind the wheel. Your road test is today. Panic sets in. You feel your brain running away from you, a brain predisposed to depression and hypomania.

Lights, camera, action ...

In 1976, I moved to New Zealand with my fiancée. Her uncle was at the airport to pick us up. I hopped in the passenger side of the car. In New Zealand the passenger side comes equipped with steering wheel and pedals and control panel. There is only a glove box on the driver's side.

I never recovered from the incident.

New Zealanders drive on the left side of the road, and they refused to make an exception for me. Most of them displayed a total lack of understanding when I entered roundabouts on the side to which I was accustomed. Plus, speed limit signs were posted in kilograms, kilobytes, whatever.

Soon, my wife was doing all the driving. I didn't bother to apply for a New Zealand license. I allowed my two North American licenses to expire. It's not like cars are important, anyway.

Eleven years in New Zealand, five in Australia. By the time I returned to the States, I had lost the will to get back behind the wheel.

Years passed ...

Then, in late 2006, I moved to rural Southern California. If I wanted to buy groceries or do my banking or fill a prescription, I needed to drive 12 miles to the nearest town. Oops, I don't drive.

A month went by. I purchased an old beater, but it sat in the front of the house for 18 months. Finally, I willed myself to do the work and obtain my California learner's permit. I got behind the wheel for the first time in decades. Nothing came back. I'd completely lost my driving reflexes. The road persisted in moving to where the car didn't want to be.

Then came the day of my road test. Compounding my usual worries was the fact that I had just met a lovely woman who lived 40 miles away. I NEEDED to pass this test.

The inspector asks me to turn on my left signal. I turn on my right signal. It's all downhill from there. FAIL! Now I'm depressed. I'm a loser, an idiot. The woman I just met is going to dump me for sure. We work it out. She will help me. I book another appointment.

Two weeks later, I call her in a panic. I've just discovered DMV videos on YouTube. More than a hundred of them. Ten top reasons drivers fail the test. Something about forgetting that Burma is now called Myanmar. Automatic fail.

I'm never going to pass this test!

Moment of truth. I've willed my heart down to 300 beats a minute. Turn left, the inspector instructs.

What did he mean by that? I wonder.

He's scribbling in his clipboard. One turn and already I've given him something to write about! I'm doomed! I see a city bus stopping. Am I supposed to stop for the bus? I turn to the inspector for an answer. Nothing. I feel extreme panic overtaking me. I freeze like a deer in the headlights.

I don't know what to do. My brain completely fails me. I really don't know what to do. I'm about to bring the car to a complete stop on a busy thoroughfare. FAIL! I know it. I just know it.

Somehow I manage to get the car back to the DMV and park it without running over any pedestrians. The inspector tells me I have a tendency to overthink and panic. Duh! He tells me I've passed. I PASSED! I refrain from hugging him.

History lesson: Howard Hughes was an aviation

pioneer, movie producer, inventor, entrepreneur, and ladies' man. But, in the prime of life, he became reduced to nothing at the prospect of simply going out the door. He couldn't do it. He never overcame it.

The prospect of driving was one of those things that reduced me to nothing. Of all the things I've been through in my life, getting back behind the wheel was by far the most terrifying. I also regard it as one of my greatest achievements. If nothing else, facing down your fears has a way of turning you into your own hero, even if others only shake their heads.

Inevitably, it's our manias and depressions that bring us to the attention of psychiatry. Anxiety, though, may be the major impediment to getting our lives back on track. Walk into any bipolar support group and you will hear people talking of how depression and mania effectively masked their anxiety. They had no idea it was there.

They found out soon enough. You can well appreciate the frustration. You set goals and just about reach them, and then—when no one's looking—our trickster god moves the goal posts.

It's even worse than that. Via the stress connection, anxiety can trigger mania, hypomania, and depression. And the presence of anxiety makes the mood episode much more difficult to contend with. In the context of mania and hypomania, imagine our thoughts running away from us. Now imagine that runaway thinking having to do with meeting a project deadline or an impending meeting with the boss.

Now imagine losing sleep over it. There is absolutely no upside to this scenario.

20. WHEN "UP" GOES WRONG, PART II:
BIPOLAR I AND MANIA

Remember that proud moment at the Thanksgiving table when you told Uncle Shithead what you really think of him and his stupid politics and where he could stick it, along with the cranberry sauce and stuffing?

It was your finest hour, no doubt about it, but for some strange reason your partner didn't congratulate you. No, on the drive back—pointedly and with great emphasis— she didn't say a word. Tacit. Allegro con silentio. Then, at home, in your pajamas, just as you were dimming the lights, she let loose. She tore into you. She ripped you to shreds, lacerated, eviscerated—folded, stapled, mutilated —pulled out a Sharpie and wrote Mongolia on the one patch of contiguous skin remaining on your forehead, affixed a stamp, and tossed you in a snowbank in the general direction of the mailbox.

I will be devoting a whole book to bipolar relationships. For the time being, this quick word: If you're the long-suffering loved one of someone with bipolar—please— never confront him or her just before bed or in bed. However much you need to stand up for yourself, however you are feeling emotionally, however justified you may be, now more than ever, this is when you need to be breathing through your nose.

I hear you. I feel your pain. Please hear me out ...

First, someone should have told off Uncle Shithead ages ago. He is the reason everyone dreads holiday gatherings in the first place. Moreover, he represents a clear and present danger to anyone whose mood episodes are triggered by stress. This is why every holiday season I let my readers know that staying home and watching CSI reruns in your pajamas may not be such a bad idea, but I digress ...

Let's assume your loved one—we'll call him Joe—was operating at the high end of hypomania. Thanks to your diplomacy, he got through the rest of the afternoon with no further incident, not counting his passionate rendering of *Beowulf* in the original Old English while everyone else was trying to watch the football game, including Uncle Shithead who is now unaccountably meek and accommodating.

Anyway ...

Somehow you managed to get your loved one home in one piece, where sleep awaits, nature's soft nurse, and what did you do? You just made sure he won't be getting any sleep tonight. As if you haven't already suffered enough, wait till you have to deal with him in the morning.

Let's back up a second. Most of us have become fairly adept in anticipating our cycles and taking the appropriate preventative action. I will be going into this in a lot more detail in a future book in this series. For right now, I urge you to Google "mindfulness" together with my last name. A whole host of articles and two videos will come up.

Basically, mindfulness is the mind watching the mind. In this context, if we can pick up our subtle changes in our thoughts and moods and behaviors and energy levels we have an excellent chance of heading off our next mood episode at the pass.

Needless to say, it is best to spot these changes while we're still in "normal," where simple and immediate solutions tend to present themselves, such as stopping to smell the roses or retiring early for the evening.

Hypomania presents more of a challenge, though

hardly an insurmountable one. At this stage, we're looking for signs of clear discomfort rather than subtle changes. We may suddenly realize that we are feeling entirely too good for our own good. Or too upset and unpleasant.

The recognition dawns: Our engine is revving too hard. Our thoughts are racing too fast, we're talking too much, thinking too big, making impulsive decisions. We look down and realize we're floating at tree-top level. Negotiating our way back to earth without crash-landing is going to take time.

Heaven help, though, if nothing has showed up on your radar. Or if ground control has failed you. It happens. Imagine this time it was a wedding you attended rather than a family Thanksgiving. There you are, unaccountably out on the dance floor, having the time of your life. Your wife is delighted.

Okay, she has to overlook the fact that you are shamelessly flirting with the five other women gyrating in your vicinity. But here you are, actually dancing. Ask yourself—how many women ever succeed in getting their men to dance with them? I rest my case.

Not only that, your performance inspires Uncle Shithead, who, it turns out, is really an old softy deep inside, and suddenly, thanks to you, everyone in the room is levitating in a Summer of Love outpouring of universal joy and harmony. The bedroom scene that night is going to be entirely different.

Who wants it to stop? Can you blame yourself? Can you blame your wife? And if you are having this kind of effect at work, who wants it to stop there, either?

So it is that in certain cases we can transit all the way through hypomania and into mania without running a single red light.

"Yeh, well it was my turn to write the paper that day," I

joked to an associate on the phone back in 1988. At the time, I was working as a financial journalist on a newspaper in Melbourne, Australia. One day, three or four of my pieces turned up on the business pages, together with my review of a Frank Sinatra concert leading the entertainment section.

When you're producing like this, who the hell is going to tell you to slow down? A month later, I would be out of a job. On my website, I go into a bit more detail how this happened, but I leave a lot out and I'm not about to flesh out the narrative here.

If I did, it would only sound like empty bragging. It would create an entirely wrong impression. Case in point …

Back in 2007, about eight months after my book *Living Well with Depression and Bipolar Disorder* came out, Julie from Oprah called. This is the type of call every author dreams of. I could see it now, Oprah, herself: "Ladies and gentlemen, today we're going to devote an entire show to the most inspirational person I ever met, author of a most wonderful book …"

But soon it became obvious why Julie was calling. She was looking for a mad scene. But my particular mad scene from way back was fairly ho-hum, as far as mad scenes go. I walked off my job. I did it without raising my voice, without threatening anyone, without speaking in tongues or having conversations with invisible people. Moreover, I was in my business attire, perfectly groomed.

Yet I was out of my mind.

I can see it now on Oprah: "The true story of the man who handed in his resignation." No, Julie would have to find someone else. Sure enough, a few weeks later, the following appeared on the front page of Oprah's website: "Did Bipolar Drive a Mother to Kill Her Child? Tune in

Monday."

If Oprah calls, tell her I'm busy.

In 2009, Maggie Reese self-published a memoir, *Runaway Mind*. Maggie, who is in her thirties, was a star distance-runner in high school and college, with an Olympic dream, one that came crashing down with a career-ending injury. Then came depression followed by madness.

If you're just skimming the book you are likely to miss the part where she describes being so amped up on mania out in Yosemite that the crowd she was hanging with wanted whatever she was on. To put this in perspective, these are the type of people who jump off cliff faces for fun.

An editor in a mainstream publishing house would have told her to expand her wacky wild times into at least four chapters, and move this part of the narrative to the front of the book. But Maggie was far more interested in writing about the hell she put her family through and the love and support they gave her every step of the way.

Maggie lives in the greater San Diego area and is active in the local mental health advocacy scene, so it was inevitable we would cross paths. On a recent occasion, we decided to meet for a burger in Mission Valley, somewhere deep in the interior of a super-complex of mega-malls bounded and bisected by three interstates, two state highways, and a galactic black hole.

In Southern California, it is best to think of freeways as obstacles you need to outwit as opposed to roads that actually take you to your destination. Maggie fully understood the state I was in.

We greeted each other from across a gulf in the parking lot. Even from a distance, I could feel a life-affirming psychic charge coming from her, one that told me I was with one of my own, that I had nothing to fear, nothing to hide.

Maggie is a generation apart from me and leads a very different life running her own businesses and raising a daughter with her school-teacher husband. Tall and athletic, exuding a buoyancy of spirit, she comes across as the woman who has it all.

Then again, when you've lost your sanity only to miraculously find it again after a long struggle, maybe that's the only impression you are capable of making. Appearances can be deceiving. We try to assume one mask to hide our vulnerability, only to discover that without our knowledge our inner strengths have slipped on a completely different persona over the one we thought we were showing to the world. I have been through many strange experiences of people describing me to me, and— I swear—it's a completely different person they are talking about.

I suspect Maggie feels the same way. In any event, out in the parking lot, our multi-layered masks instantly come off. It's just her and me and our respective psychic charges. Call it bands of light. There we are, two beings with little in common yet everything in common, laughing, joking, opening up, talking about the sorts of things we would never dare tell another person, not even those closest to us.

Over burgers, we can't shut up. Too soon, it's time to go, she to her life, me to mine.

A couple of years earlier, we had met on a different occasion. Then, I was serving on the board of our local NAMI (National Alliance for the Mentally Ill). Maggie was to be the recipient of our Young Advocate of the Year Award. She would be honored at our annual dinner, along with five others.

The local mental health community packed out the hotel ballroom. Seated at one of the front tables was Maggie's family—father, mother, siblings—down from northern California. Up on stage, it wasn't about the award. You saw it in Maggie's face, the way she looked toward her family.

An hour or so later, I was standing in a near-empty ballroom. The house lights were on, the tables cleared. I spotted Maggie and her family, heading toward the door. I rushed over and congratulated her and introduced myself to her family.

Suddenly, we were all rooted to the floor. The family had to talk. They needed to talk. I felt a need to listen. Rather, I felt privileged to listen. It was one of those rare moments.

Read enough obituaries and you will come across, "after a brave battle with …" Go into any hospital gift shop and there are bouquets and balloons. But for mental illness, there are no baubles, no balloons, no bar-coded badges of courage. Life is difficult as it is without calling attention to ourselves. For patients and family members alike, we feel only shame, even in our finest hours.

This was not one of those occasions. I'm guessing that my presence provided Maggie's family confirmation, particularly for her parents, that it was okay to take pride in their daughter, not for the races they expected her to win, but for the one they hardly anticipated, the important one—the race for her life. It was a family effort, a family affair. And this night, of all nights, a roomful of people were actually applauding. In this upside-down world of ours, when things occasionally go right, we have to kick ourselves to ensure we're not dreaming.

Maggie and her good friend.

21. WHEN "UP" GOES WRONG, PART III: PSYCHOSIS AND SCHIZOAFFECTIVE

Although mania is a fairly rare event, it governs the entire bipolar conversation. Even if you only had one manic episode in your life, psychiatry regards you as bipolar I forever. Even if your highs top out at hypomania—which is the case for those with bipolar II—or even if your last mania was decades in the past, your doctor is bound to recommend a mood-stabilizing medication to keep you out of mania, most likely a cocktail of meds.

You can prove your doctor wrong by seeing how things go on no meds, but would you want to bet your life on it? Such is the bipolar's dilemma.

So terrifying is the specter of a recurrence into mania that most patients willingly do what their doctors tell them. Thus, contrary to conventional wisdom, we stay on our meds precisely because the very thought of losing control strikes the fear of God into us. Yes, there are serious issues with meds non-adherence, but to wrap it in a narrative of patient-fault is entirely misleading.

This is an extremely involved issue, including the fact that there are people who do very well on meds-free regimens, which we will go into at length in a future book. For now, my bottom line has always been this:

In the initial going and for some time after, you may have to put up with onerous medication side effects. But emergency medication and getting you stable should not be confused with long-term treatment. Over the long-haul, there is no justification for you having to put up with side effects that only militate against your recovery or that rob you of your personality, your sense of being you.

Keeping you out of the hospital is not a treatment plan, nor a legitimate goal. Getting you back to where you were before—or where you wish to go from here—is. Doctors will give lip service to this, but nearly all of them tend to err on the side of overmedicating us.

On the other hand, can we blame them?

Back in 2012, I drove across town to hear Maricela Estrada give a talk hosted by the International Bipolar Foundation. A couple of years earlier, she had self-published a book, *Bipolar Girl: My Psychotic Self*.

I arrived early and thus had a chance to have a one-on-one conversation. Maricela is in her early 30s and is employed as a medical case worker for the Department of Mental Health in LA. She has an engaging manner and a delightfully bubbly personality, and in no time we were laughing and joking.

She experienced her first episode as a school girl and has survived numerous suicide attempts, not to mention a drive-by shooting where a bullet whizzed past her head as she was lying in bed. The depressions continued through high school, but could not extinguish her irrepressible high spirits. She was very popular as a student, involved in activities, and elected prom queen.

Things fell apart soon after graduation. Mania, psychotic breaks, more suicide attempts, hospitalizations. During stable periods she managed to hold down various jobs and excel in college. But then she would go off her meds and things would unravel. One time, in a car in a parking lot, she was convinced the world was ending. She heard a chorus of angels. She started screaming at people, and stripped off her blouse in order to be as naked as Adam and Eve. She was apprehended and handcuffed and put into a police car, breasts exposed.

In due course Maricela ended her denial and accepted

the fact that she needed to stay on her meds. The meds were no picnic, but eventually she found a regimen she could tolerate.

Maricela and her stylish friend.

In case you're wondering, psychosis is about as bad as it gets. Even in severe mania, one can argue, we can at least discern a tenuous connection to reality. In psychosis, we get the impression of the mind breaking free of reality's gravitational field. The condition may exist as a stand-alone entity, but it is most associated with schizophrenia, where it is a core feature. In the context of mood disorders, we get the impression it is hitching a ride on depression and mania.

Back in the old days, psychosis was virtually interchangeable with "insanity." These days, we identify the term with hallucinations and delusional thinking. In some cases, we may see a breakdown in personal identity.

Now that I've scared the crap out of you, it is perfectly normal to feel a sense of disorientation a good deal of the time. Our neural circuits hardly process simultaneous sensory information at the same uniform speed, much less to the same level of completion. Our brain, to compensate, is constantly filling in the blanks, adjusting, anticipating, often seeing and hearing what is not there.

Just one example: The "blind spot" of the retina contains no photoreceptors. The brain literally Photoshops a more complete picture. What we "see" is only a representation of what we think we see.

On top of that, we are screening this information through the complex filter of our own fears and desires and cognitive biases. Basically, we have constructed a working reality that gets us through the day. It's how the healthy brain works. But it would be a mistake to view this as an objective bitmap reproduction of our environment.

Seen this way, it is easy to see how distortions in one's personal reality may develop. It's happened to all of us— our food takes on an unaccountable metallic tang, we swear we hear people talking, and so on. Then reality— our personalized version—resets to normal and we think no more of it.

But imagine if things go wrong.

In her highly acclaimed 2007 book, *The Center Cannot Hold*, Elyn Saks recounts how as a graduate student at Oxford she caught herself talking to herself on the street and didn't regard this as strange. Things went downhill from there. Nevertheless, with professional help, she managed to hold herself together and complete her degree, taking four years instead of two.

Dr Saks was diagnosed with schizophrenia, but it took her a full two decades to reach a state of acceptance. As she wrote in a January 23, 2013 op-ed piece in the *New York Times*:

My prognosis was "grave": I would never live independently, hold a job, find a loving partner, get married. My home would be a board-and-care facility, my days spent watching TV in a day room with other people debilitated by mental illness. I would work at menial jobs when my symptoms were quiet.

Today, she is a chaired professor of law at USC, plus an adjunct in psychiatry at UCSD, plus is on the faculty of the New Center for Psychoanalysis in LA, and is married. In her book, she described her first romantic kiss in lord knows when. "It was fantastic," she wrote. "It was even better than getting an article published."

In 1899, Emil Kraepelin brought order to psychiatry by separating out manic-depression from what he called "dementia praecox," which he viewed as an irreversible cognitive disintegration. His followers changed the name to schizophrenia to imply a better prognosis.

In his 1921 *Manic-Depressive Insanity*, Kraepelin noted that delusions may occur in mania, "usually in a more jocular way." This accords with the modern conception of "mood-congruent" features, such as seeing oneself as descended from royalty. Delusions congruent with depression, on the other hand, "frequently exist in the closest connection with the delusion of sin."

Seriously, a whole century of his successors can't top that.

Psychiatrists in Europe and America readily adopted Kraepelin's manic-depression/schizophrenia split, though not always in ways the old master would have imagined, and the early DSMs did little to instill diagnostic confidence. One problem involved patients who seemed to fall into the so-called gap between manic-depression and schizophrenia.

The DSMs I and II categorized "schizoaffective" as a

"type" of schizophrenia. The DSM III upgraded the condition to a "disorder," profusely apologized for lack of a checklist, and simply urged clinicians to make the diagnosis when they couldn't decide between a mood disorder or schizophrenia. This is how clinicians still operate for the most part.

If the patient happens to be African-American, by the way, one guess what doctors decide. Please, don't make me cite the studies.

As a rough guide, on one side of the divide, we have DSM acknowledgement that psychotic features can occur in bipolar mania and depression and in unipolar depression. The understanding is that the psychosis is part and parcel of the mood episode. In other words, in bipolar, where there is no mood episode there should be no psychosis.

The implication is you can manage psychosis by managing your moods.

Over on the other side, we have acknowledgement that mood episodes may exist in schizophrenia, but these are a sideshow compared to the main event of disordered thinking and behavior. Psychosis is viewed as part and parcel of a major cognitive malfunction rather than bearing any relation to mood. Clinicians tend to look for delusions of the more bizarre variety, "incongruent" with mood.

Also, compared to the more fleeting psychoses associated with bipolar, delusions in schizophrenia may go on for years on end.

So far, so good. As to what lies in the middle ...

The DSM appears to view schizoaffective as a hybrid, one that incorporates "schizophrenia lite" combined with bipolar I. The disordered thinking and behavior associated with schizophrenia are evident, but not with the same severity and duration. Clinicians also look for evidence of psychosis occurring without the mood episode. In effect, the psychosis is free-floating.

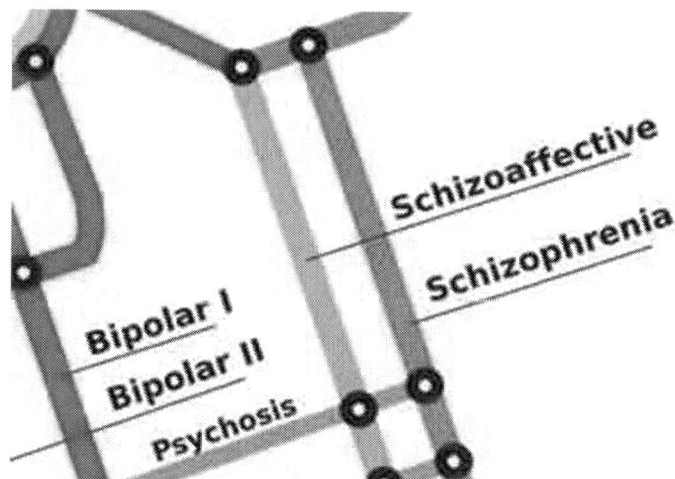

Map of reality close-up 12: It's easiest to conceive of bipolar as a mood disorder and schizophrenia as a thought disorder. But then we have what looks like a hybrid presence in the middle. To make matters even more confusing, psychosis cuts across the entire spectrum, from schizophrenia to mania to depression.

All well and good, but everything breaks down in the real world. Just a slight alteration in presentation from one psychiatric visit to the next can change the diagnosis. Indeed, the schizoaffective diagnosis simply doesn't hold over steady the course of a lifetime.

This is one good reason why Kraepelin was no fan of symptom lists. Instead, he placed greater stock in keeping meticulous records, recording family history, and observing patients over long periods of time. By contrast, a psychiatric resident trying to parse the fine points of differential diagnosis on someone the police have just brought in off the street doesn't have the luxury of long-term observation. Neither do the follow-up clinicians.

The academic food fights are legion. On one hand, there is universal consensus that we need to better account for patients with mood disorders who have psychosis to contend with, including those patients who wind up in the middle of the diagnostic divide. On the other, there is no point of agreement on how to go about it.

In mid-2006, at a session of the International Society of Bipolar Disorders conference in Edinburgh, the conversation started to get particularly interesting. Nick Craddock of Cardiff University was discussing genetic susceptibility to psychosis.

Someone mentioned Kraepelin one time too many, and the frustration in his response was evident. The gist of his remarks amounted to something along these lines: Why the fascination with Kraepelin? You don't hear historical figures referred to with such reverence in other branches of medicine. Other branches of medicine work with hard science.

In an article in the June 2007 *World Psychiatry*, Dr Craddock summarily dispatched the old master: A discussion of Kraepelin, he wrote, "is not of direct relevance to contemporary clinical psychiatry."

Dr Craddock has a point, but the field is a long way off from making a definitive diagnostic call based on a brain scan or gene scan or lab assay. Or, for that matter, in coming up with a whole new classification system based on brain physiology. Even one day in the distant future when the field eventually meets the exacting white coat standards of say cardiology, for the reasons Dr Andreasen cited in an earlier chapter, it would be foolhardy to toss aside the wisdom so laboriously gained from the efforts of the old masters.

Kraepelin never had access to a brain scan machine, but in his detailed descriptions of his patients, we can literally imagine him peering into their grey matter. We see his subjects not as voxels on a brain scan monitor or as anomalous alleles along some stretch of DNA, but as people with identities. Even separated by a century, they are so real to us that when the old master brings up the topic of suicide, we catch ourselves recoiling in sympathetic concern.

As to our current real people: Maricela is the story of a woman who has fallen down seven times and picked herself up eight. Dr Saks battled against an inhumane mental health system that was all too happy to write her off. Both are doing very well. Both have found meds that work for them.

But deep in our gut we also know that the battle is never over. One snap of a thread, one straw too many, one prank of a trickster god—then things fall apart. The center cannot hold. With recovery, as with life, there are no happy endings, only an endless succession of beginnings, each with their special terms and conditions, each with their new sets of demands.

We have picked ourselves up more times than we have fallen, but what about next time? We are a walking mass of contradictions—strong and courageous and resourceful, but also vulnerable. That is one of the lessons we can all learn from listening to people like Maricela and Dr Saks. We can cheer their considerable triumphs, but at the same time we are holding our collective breath.

Update: In August 2015, at its annual conference, the National Alliance for Mental Illness (NAMI) honored Maricela with its Outstanding Peer Award.

22. REVIEWING "UP"

An occupational hazard in writing about bipolar is that, despite our best efforts, description and reality are never going to quite match. When dogma intervenes—as first in the case of Freud and later the DSM—we witness severe disconnects.

One cognitive trap we fall into has something to do with Plato's ideal forms. In his 2007 book, *The Concepts of Psychiatry*, and in numerous think pieces, Nassir Ghaemi dons his philosopher's hat and challenges his fellow psychiatrists to question their own reasoning.

So let's talk about Plato's ideal forms for a bit. Here's the deal:

Every object or concept here on earth is inherently imperfect, but they all have their ideal counterparts existing on a different plane. Thus, the perfect circle, the perfect tree, the perfect hamburger. According to Plato, in his Allegory of the Cave, the objects we see are not real. They are merely shadowy expressions of their ideal forms.

All well and good. But what if the ideal forms we imagine in our heads blind us to what is going on here on earth? Dr Ghaemi cites the example of conventional psychiatry for the better part of a century failing to recognize mixed states, such was its fixation on the ideal forms of "pure" manias and depressions.

We can take this a step further with the DSM's simplistic split into an idealized form of unipolar depression and idealized bipolar disorder.

Below represents bipolar in its ideal form—equal parts depression and mania. You will see many versions of this all over the internet.

The reality, though, is much closer to this, with depression as the dominant presence.

But we're still hopelessly lost in Platoland. A true representation would look more like a jagged coastline with land and sea in a perpetual tug of war. Salty marshes deep inland, sand bars and rocky outcrops defying the ocean. Zoom in to the tidal pools or floating plankton or grains of sand and we uncover whole new micro-universes. On and on …

Bipolar, like everything else in the world, is fractal and chaotic. But to explain it, we need to employ ideal forms. In portraying bipolar as a cycling illness, I too fall into Plato's trap. But my ideal cycle, I submit, lasts as long as a quantum phenomenon under the steely gaze of Warner Heisenberg. We're back to uncertainty and infinite complexity.

This concludes Part III on mapping up. To summarize:

- It is easiest to regard bipolar as a cycling illness characterized by recurring depressions broken up by intervals of "up."
- "Up" is anything higher than "down."

- "Up" loosely falls into mania, hypomania, and "normal."
- Up is extremely subjective. One person's hypomania may be another person's "normal." Our clinicians may not appreciate this.
- Where "up" tops out at "normal," we may be looking at highly recurrent depression, which Goodwin and Jamison and others would place on the bipolar spectrum. The DSM, however, regards this form of depression as strictly unipolar.
- The bipolar spectrum includes a vast population of those with sub-threshold hypomania symptoms. The DSM pays regard to this with the "Other Specified" (formerly NOS) classification.
- Nevertheless, the fate of these patients is to be misdiagnosed with unipolar depression and put on the wrong treatments.
- Where "up" tops out at hypomania, we are looking at bipolar II, which only achieved DSM recognition in 1994. Hypomania is highly subjective. What may be normal to one person may be a major concern for another. This brings us into considerations of "state" vs "trait" and a discussion of temperament.
- Thus, the state of hypomania and the traits of hyperthymia—knowing which is your own personal "which" will help you find your true "normal."
- Needless to say, teasing out isolated instances of hypomania poses extreme challenges to arriving at a correct bipolar II diagnosis. This is compounded by our inability to recall when we ever felt better than normal while in a depressed state.

- On its own, hypomania is not a pathological state. In some instances, it may come across as the type of personality makeover we are all longing for. But it also tends to take us out of our comfort zone, which can lead to considerable distress and behavior resulting in bad consequences. Also, hypomania may foreshadow mania, which is a huge worry.
- Where "up" tops out at mania, we have bipolar I. Mania may be the trademark state for bipolar, the one that defines treatment, but it is also fairly rare. Most of the time, "up" is likely to top out at "normal" or hypomania—but you never know.
- Hypomania and mania can also turn dysphoric. These are mixed states which can best be described as road rage, even if you're not driving.
- Mixed anxiety states are also common, not to mention pure anxiety. For our purposes, it is best to think of anxiety as a mood state, worthy of the same status as depression and mania and hypomania.
- As if things are already not complicated enough, we have the phenomenon of psychosis, which can best be described as a break from reality. These breaks run the gamut from mild to severe. In a bipolar context, psychosis appears to attach to depression or mania and bears a certain congruency to the current mood state. In schizophrenia, psychosis is free-floating and generally incongruent with mood.
- Then there is the hybrid diagnosis of schizoaffective, one that presents like bipolar, but with free-floating psychotic features. The real-world difficulties in parsing out diagnostic fine

points on live patients leads to no end of academic food fights.

Let's move on to depression ...

PART FOUR: MAPPING DOWN

My life, being made of four, with two alone
  Sinks down to death, oppressed with melancholy;

  —Shakespeare, Sonnet XLV

23. DEPRESSION: WHAT IS IT?

On average, we spend far more of our time in depression than we do in mania or hypomania—by a ratio of three to one for those with bipolar I, according to a major 2003 study. Estimates go much higher for those with bipolar II.

This was news to me when I first heard Robert Post, then at the NIMH, give us a preview of his findings at the Fourth International Conference on Bipolar Disorder in Pittsburgh in 2001. The fact that he felt obliged to report this meant it was also news to the 500 or so clinicians and researchers in the room.

At the time, I was into my third year of my bipolar diagnosis. Until then, I had simply assumed that I was some kind of diagnostic oddball—this depressed person who couldn't be counted on to flip into mania when I was supposed to, a walking black hole, no fun to have around. Why did I always have to be so different?

But now Dr Post was telling me I was normal, at least by bipolar standards. Basically, we are the death of the party, and in this regard I fit right in. Believe it or not, this came as good news to me.

Some people may experience being up more than down, and in rare cases some may never know what it's like to just want to go to sleep and never wake up. But as a general rule it is much more helpful to regard bipolar as simply another form of depression. With a bit of a stretch, we can argue that is how Kraepelin saw it, too.

But it's easy to anticipate resistance to this notion. Why, for instance, should someone whose idea of a wacky wild time out on the town involves coupon night at the Olive Garden be regarded the same as someone splashing naked in a public fountain?

But that is exactly the wrong question to ask. The more relevant query is what do these two individuals have in common? The answer, of course, is their depressions. Our depressions. Because we are down way more than up, we can make a strong case that depression is by far the more disabling, not to mention lethal, part of our illness.

Earth to psychiatry: Our ups don't define us. Rather, we're brothers and sisters in depression. If these depressions run a highly recurrent course, then we're practically identical twins.

Let's put it this way: If you are depressed, then performing your day job is going to be highly problematic. So is maintaining relationships. So is being at peace (or at least in a state of ccasc-fire) with yourself. We need our wits about us merely to survive in this world. But— gradually or suddenly—it's as if our brains have quit on us. We can't cope, we can't function.

Depression is a Stone Age condition, a very modern phenomenon. There is no allowance in a post-industrial service economy for an individual who is not on his or her game. A teacher keeping 30 kids under control is fully dependent on an operational brain. A journalist racing to meet a deadline needs to do it with all his neurons firing. A salesperson requires every chunk of available grey matter to make it look as if she is glad to see you.

On top of that, these same individuals require full processing speed to manage their personal lives and family obligations. So much to do, so little time to do it in. Maybe we can write off one bad day. Two bad days is going to get the attention of people who rely on you. Two weeks of bad days is catastrophic.

Basically, we KNOW when we are depressed. We SENSE something is wrong. We literally FEEL our brains quitting on us. At the same time, though, we tend to be in denial. We think that if only we were stronger, if only we had the strength of character to snap out of it, we will be fine. In the meantime, our depression-fueled inner mother-in-law is telling us that we only have ourselves to blame.

Generally, it's only when our lives have fallen apart that we seek help, but even then our denial is strong. Typically, we will complain to our general practitioners of physical symptoms. A smart GP will take the time to probe for mental symptoms, but who has time?

Eventually, though, a GP or psychiatrist will make the obvious call—depression. At last, you have a name for it, the source of all your woes. Or do you?

"Depression isn't the word for it," were the very first words I wrote in what would be my new career as a mental health journalist. The term is merely a medical confirmation that your brain has lost—at least for the time being—its capacity to fully handle whatever life may be throwing your way. Now that you know that you are "depressed," you need to find out what is really going on.

Back in 2004, I came across a journal article by Gordon Parker of the University of New South Wales. In the article, Dr Parker noted that in clinical trials, drug companies lump all depressed patients together, regardless of age, gender, or symptoms. Not surprisingly, trial results for the test treatment are only slightly better than the placebo—good enough for an FDA indication and a drug company license to print money, but eminently unsuited to offer a clinician or a patient any real guidance.

According to Dr Parker, in a 2007 piece:

Depression is a diagnosis that will remain a non-specific "catch all" until common sense brings current confusion to order. As the

American journalist Ed Murrow observed in another context:
"Anyone who isn't confused doesn't really understand the situation."

Similarly, in a 2013 journal editorial, Nassir Ghaemi and his co-authors attacked psychiatry's view of depression, noting that the DSM version is so wide as to be virtually meaningless. According to Dr Ghaemi:

The traditional analogy of antidepressant usage for depression to insulin usage to diabetes may be wrong-headed: Depression is not a single disease entity ...

A study appearing in the Oct 2014 *Journal of Affective Disorders* sheds further light. In the study, Eiko Fried of the University of Leuven in Belgium and Randolf Nesse of Arizona State University broke down data from STAR*D, an NIMH-underwritten real-world trial of antidepressants.

Some background ...

Over the early 2000s, STAR*D recruited about 3,700 "depressed" patients. In the first round of the trials, about half the subjects showed short-term improvement on the antidepressant Celexa. This was to be expected.

In the second round, the researchers applied other options on the non-responders, including a different class of antidepressant and various meds combos. Some of the patients showed improvement. Again, the result ran according to expectations.

The third round produced the real surprise: A failure on two consecutive antidepressants virtually predicted failure on a third. Twelve-month results were totally discouraging: Those who showed promising short-term outcomes tended to relapse over the long-term.

The principal researchers in the study struggled

mightily to put a positive spin on the data, but their own numbers told a different story. As Dr Ghaemi wrote in a Feb 2009 blog on *Psychology Today*:

> *Further, and perhaps most humblingly, even if antidepressants worked in the short term (2 months ...), one-half of patients who stayed on them relapsed into depression within one year. At the one year outcome, only about 25% of patients actually had remained well on and tolerated an antidepressant, much below the levels most clinicians seem to feel occurs in their clinical experience.*

It is tempting to use the STAR*D findings to condemn antidepressants wholesale. More realistically, we need to question our whole notion of depression, which is Dr Ghaemi's point. Until we know what we're dealing with, we will have no idea how to go about treating it. This brings us back to our Fried and Nesse study:

In recruiting their patients for STAR*D, the original researchers screened their subjects using the QIDS rating scale, which tests for 12 symptoms. Taking a second look at the data, Drs Fried and Nesse found, on average, the subjects exhibited six symptoms, the most common being sad mood, loss of energy, and concentration problems.

In theory, the different combinations of symptoms would yield more than a thousand unique profiles, and that is what Drs Fried and Nesse found—1030 with an average of 3.6 individuals per profile (nearly half with just one person per profile). Even their attempts at lumping together similar symptom profiles showed wide diversity (what the experts refer to as heterogeneity).

The quick takeaway is that not all depressions are the same,—very different, in fact. Which is why—to freely editorialize—STAR*D was doomed from the get-go. Back in the early 2000s, it seemed like a good idea to treat

3,700 individuals as if they were all the same, with the expectation that if we just kept throwing antidepressants at them they would all eventually get better, some on their first antidepressant treatment, others on their second or third or fourth.

A decade later, it is easy to see the absurdity in that proposition. "Depression" is obviously not one disease. It is not even one disease with numerous manifestations. If that were the case, we would have had our one magic bullet by now, equivalent to an antibiotic or a decongestant or other class of drug. The pill would target the true underlying biological target, and the symptoms— whatever they may be—would simply go away.

It's true that physical medicine enjoys an advantage that psychiatry doesn't of making an accurate diagnosis based on high technology. Even accounting for that, however, there is no excuse for psychiatry treating every depression as the same, as the equivalent of "runny nose disease" or "stomach ache disease." We still have the power to differentiate based on what we can observe, and until psychiatry makes some credible attempts in this direction we will continue to remain mired in ignorance. As Drs Fried and Nesse conclude: We need to acknowledge that major depression "is not one coherent condition with a single cause."

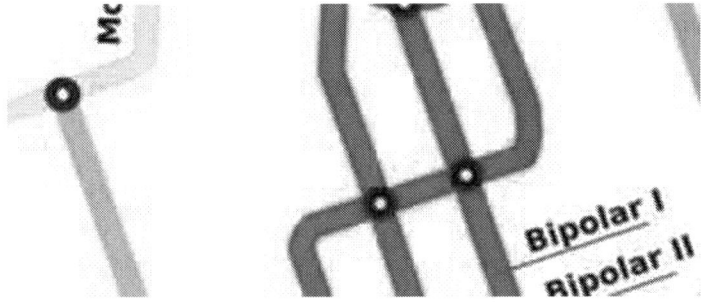

Map of reality close-up 13: What the hell is it? Note how the three dark lines representing recurrent depression, bipolar II, and bipolar I bear a close relationship to each other, even criss-crossing at one point to suggest that in some instances recurrent depression may be bipolar waiting to happen.

Now take a look at that lighter line way off to the left. This represents chronic depression. The DSM regards both chronic and recurrent depression both as part of the unipolar phenomenon. If this were a DSM map, then, we would see only two red lines The catch, though, is that no one has a clue what unipolar is, other than it does not include mania. But that doesn't stop doctors from diagnosing it and prescribing antidepressants for it.

24. DEPRESSION: IT'S COMPLICATED, JUST ASK LINCOLN

In the spring of 2008, while in Washington DC to attend a psychiatric conference, I visited the Lincoln Memorial with two friends. It was evening. Against the floodlights, the building fairly glowed. I stepped out of the car and suddenly I felt like a pilgrim visiting a sacred shrine. If ever there were an American saint, it was our sixteenth President.

"I am now the most miserable man living," the 31-year-old Lincoln confessed.

Depression was a constant in Lincoln's life. He never overcame it, he never rose above it. But Joshua Wolf Shenk's 2005 *Lincoln's Melancholy* makes a compelling case that crushing depression made both the man and the President. According to Mr Shenk, depression turned Lincoln into both a hard-headed realist and allowed him to think like a visionary. It also imbued him with a higher wisdom and deeper humanity.

With malice toward none, with charity for all, with firmness in the right, as God gives us to see the right, let us strive on to finish the work we are in, to bind up the nation's wounds.

The finest words ever uttered in the English language. There they were, incised for eternity. I stood in front of his statue, massive head tilted down toward me. A school kid behind me remarked, "He looks so sad."

His first depression came as a young man in 1838. Three years later, he would experience his second. Mr Shenk reports that in January 1841, Lincoln was confined to his bed and in the care of a physician. The standard medical treatment of the day involved purging the body by aggressively drawing blood, ingesting mercury and other poisons, inducing vomiting, starving the patient, and plunging him in cold water.

Obviously, except possibly for the cold water treatment, this would not have done Lincoln much good. But would he have done better on an antidepressant? Or would the drug have flipped him into mania? According to Mr Shenk, these two depressive episodes together would suffice for a modern clinician to make a diagnosis of recurrent major depression.

Was Lincoln, then, on the bipolar spectrum? We know he loved to joke and tell tall tales. Could this be taken as evidence of "up?" Or was this his way of medicating his misery? What you might call the sad clown syndrome.

Or did it point to an anomaly—such as perking up at good news, even while feeling miserable—part of what the DSM refers to as "atypical depression"?

Just to confuse you even more, we need to ask ourselves what else was going on in Lincoln's life at the time. For one, his two early depressions occurred in the chill of winter. A winter depression? What we today refer to as seasonal affective disorder?

What else was happening? We know that his first depression more or less coincided with his grieving the loss of a dear woman companion, and the second an economic collapse that pretty much scuttled his promising political career. A more hardy soul would have shrugged off these setbacks, but maybe his sensitive nature made him vulnerable to stress.

Or maybe the hardships and grief of his tough childhood caught up to him.

Yet this same man—who so miserably fell apart on at

least two occasions and exhibited massive despair on numerous others—proved a steady hand in leading his divided nation through its worst crisis, even in the midst of a heart-rending family tragedy.

How do you explain that?

Equally important from our perspective is the fact that even during his years in the political wilderness, he led a successful middle-class life, with a flourishing law practice, a stable marriage (though to a woman who caused him numerous problems), high community standing, and no shortage of friends.

How was this possible? And how, with such crushing depressions, did one man possess the motivation to seek the highest office in the land in the first place?

Recall how in our discussion of "up" I kept urging you to keep things simple? "Up" only had to be higher than "down." Now, in our discussion of "down," I am calling for the very opposite. Rather than simple, I am asking you to think of "down" as enormously complicated. We think we know what depression is, but we only have to look at the life of Lincoln to realize that even the experts have only the slightest idea what they are talking about.

"So—can anyone here give me a one-sentence description for depression?"

In 2010, I asked this to a roomful of experts—the real experts—patients and loved ones. I was delivering a talk in Manhattan, Kansas to a conference hosted by DBSA Kansas.

"It sucks," came the first response.

"A deep dark hole," came another.

"Like having two Doberman Pinschers waiting for you to get out of bed in the morning. You aren't going anywhere."

I got someone to start writing down the answers:

"It's like you're worthless."

"You're on a raft, in the middle of a huge ocean, you can't see any land anywhere, on any horizon, and you're totally becalmed."

"It's like trying to walk through mud up to your neck."

I added one of my own—agitation and anger, a feeling of road rage. I observed a lot of nodding heads. More responses …

"I just don't want to be here anymore."

"I told my doctor a while back, I'm not suicidal; I'm homicidal."

"I think especially for a lot of guys, it's withdrawal and grouchiness."

I added one more—lack of motivation, total apathy.

I asked how many had heard of the DSM. Everyone had. "Great," I said. "Now, as you know, the DSM is a piece of fiction put out by the American Psychiatric Association."

Unlike psychiatrists and clinicians, patients and loved ones laugh at your jokes. They're engaged. They nod their heads in sympathy. They support you. I was having a great time. I really need to get out more often.

"As you may recall," I said, "there is the world-famous symptom list. You know, five of nine symptoms. But first, you have to have one of two, okay? So get this—I'm going to read this out—here's number one, for depression":

Depressed mood most of the day.

"I'm trying to figure the logic here," I confessed. "Describe depression to me. Depression is—depressed mood most of the day. Have you ever tried to describe what carrots taste like to someone who hasn't had carrots? Oh, carrots, you know, carrots—they taste like carrots."

Right, that really tells me a lot. I'm depressed. And I'm depressed because—I'm depressed. "But what is my state of mind?" I asked. "What are my feelings? What are my emotions? What are my moods?"

The DSM does give the example in "depressed most of the day" of feeling sad. "But does depression equal sad?" I asked. Well, maybe the other symptoms can help us out. The second symptom, the other one of that "one of two" is:

Loss of pleasure. "We're kind of getting there a little bit," I acknowledged. Too bad about the next four:

Weight loss or weight gain. "Oh, great, so everyone who goes to Weight Watchers is depressed."

Insomnia or hypersomnia. "That's not telling us much."

Psychomotor agitation. "So we walk funny."

Fatigue or loss of energy. "You get tired at two o'clock. Big deal."

"I'm no expert," I said. "I'm a patient just like you. But I do know how to count. So we've got nine symptoms on the list, and make that eight because that first one is just too ridiculous for words. So, we've got eight symptoms, and we only need five to cross the diagnostic threshold for a diagnosis."

And four symptoms are physical. We eat too much or too little. Same with sleep. We walk funny. We get tired. "Fine-fine-fine," I said. "So does the entire rest of the human race. Tell us something different. Tell us what friggin' state our minds are in. Tell us our thoughts, feelings, and emotions."

The DSM does mention: *Guilt or worthlessness, loss of concentration, suicidality.* "Is that it?"

"No wonder no one can help us," I said. "No one has even bothered to open up the hood and look in. So, get this. You people here, turning out on a Saturday, in Kansas ..." I turned to the person who was taking down audience responses. "Do you want to read out the list here?

"It sucks," she read. "Deep dark hole. Like two Doberman Pinschers waiting for you to get out of bed in the morning. You're worthless. On a raft in the middle of the ocean, not going anywhere, totally becalmed. Like walking in mud up to your neck. A feeling of road rage. Just don't want to be here anymore. I'm not suicidal, I'm homicidal. Withdrawal and grouchiness. Apathy, lack of motivation."

"Is that a better list than the DSM list?" I asked. "Congratulations—you guys have beat the best psychiatrists in the world. Give yourselves a round of applause."

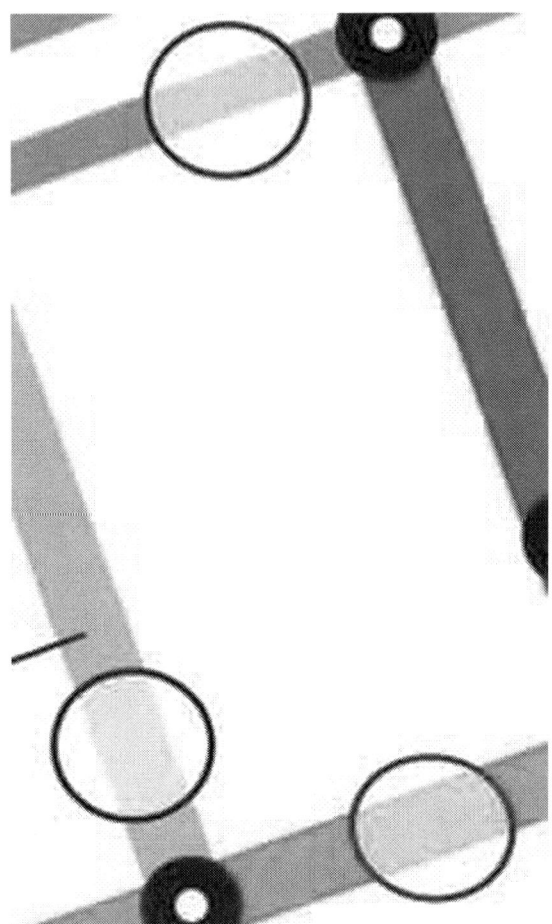

Map of reality, close-up 14: Depression is immensely complicated, but we will make an attempt at coherence by looking at the condition from three different perspectives. The bottom horizontal line represents personality/temperament, where we examine depression as part of our true "normal." The left vertical line represents chronic depression, which we will regard as unipolar. The top horizontal line represents bipolar depression.

25. DEPRESSED OR THINKING DEEP?

Author and blogger and mother of two Therese Borchard always has a way of making me feel that on a planet of seven billion strangers I have at least one person I can talk to. In November 2009 blog post on *PsychCentral*, she began:

> *I spent my adolescence and teenage years obsessing about this question: Am I depressed or just deep?*
>
> *When I was nine, I figured that I was a young Christian mystic because I related much more to the saints who lived centuries ago than to other nine-year-old girls who had crushes on boys. I couldn't understand how my sisters could waste quarters on a stupid video game when there were starving kids in Cambodia. Hello? Give them to UNICEF!*
>
> *Now I look back with tenderness to the hurting girl I was and wished somebody had been able to recognize that I was very depressed.*

See what I mean? I just know that had we been in the same class at grade school, while the other kids played ball during recess, Therese and I would have found a quiet spot to sit under a shade tree, sharing cookies our moms packed, and discussing how Augustine of Hippo must have felt after Alaric the Visigoth sacked Rome in 410 AD.

So, what was it? Were Therese and I two sensitive souls waxing philosophical, or two depressives acting strange? Therese cites Peter Kramer, author of *Against Depression* (from a 2005 *New York Times Magazine* piece), in support of the proposition that depression and thinking deep are

161

clearly distinct. Says Dr Kramer:

We idealize depression, associating it with perceptiveness, interpersonal sensitivity and other virtues. Like tuberculosis in its day, depression is a form of vulnerability that even contains a measure of erotic appeal.

First the ancient Greeks, then Renaissance thinkers, and later the Romantic movement assigned spiritual and artistic and even heroic virtues to melancholy. Nonsense, Dr Kramer responds. "Depression is not a perspective. It is a disease."

If I interpret Therese correctly in her blog piece, she found comfort in this. It came as a great relief to her to realize that her capacity to think deep, even at a young age, although unusual, was not pathological.

I, on the other hand, have an entirely different reaction. "Wait!" I want to scream at Dr Kramer. "You mean my depressions have all been for nothing?" My lost hours, lost days, entire lost years, a lost life practically, served no useful purpose whatsoever?

Screw you, Kramer! I want to keep screaming for no logical reason, whatsoever. Something that took so much from me, so much out of my life, I demand some kind of return—Jedi powers, a mystical third eye, roll-over phone minutes, whatever.

Yes, Dr Kramer is right, but so is everyone else. When it comes to the enduring question—Who the hell am I?—we are all struggling to find the truth.

You will recall that Kraepelin observed an apparent overlap between mood states and personality traits. A depressive personality, for instance, tends to give rise to depressive episodes. In other words, for many people, mild depression may be their true "normal." Imagine, for instance, recovering from the mother of all depressions only to find yourself bogged down in one of her offspring?

Psychiatry refers to this as "secondary depression," a minor depression following a major one. But is it a true depression?

A number of experts have made a case for "depressive personality disorder" (DPD). According to personality disorders expert Michael Bagby of the University of Toronto, at a session at the 2006 APA annual meeting in Toronto, those with depressive traits "may define a group who are pessimistic, disaffected, and frustrated, perhaps because they see their illness as an intractable and enduring part of their selves."

To interject briefly, here: Pessimism has its obvious downsides, but it may also take a constructive turn in the form of "depressive realism." You might describe depressive realism as the antidote to cockeyed optimism and wishful thinking. According to Joshua Wolf Shenk, Lincoln's inerrant knack for anticipating the worst may have amounted to the Union's secret weapon.

Perhaps it also helped account for his successful life. Evolutionary psychologists agree there has to be some kind of adaptive purpose to depression, the most obvious being this: If mania got our distant ancestors out and about during the warm seasons, then depression was about our conservation of energy during the cold ones, when survival demanded we stay close to our caves.

You might call depressive realism a more sophisticated version of our conservation-of-energy survival gear—the wisdom to know when to let go and cut our losses and move on, together with the foresight to spot trouble before it happens.

Evolutionary biologists talk in terms of "trade-offs." Thus, depression may confer tremendous personal strengths, but at considerable cost. We may not be Lincoln. We may only see the downside of our depressions, which is extremely logical owing to our depressed temperaments. But let's fight against type for just two seconds to consider the possibility of a modest upside.

Psychiatry—and you can argue justifiably so—does not see depression this way. Thus, even if we view depression as part of our personality, it is seen in the context of a "disorder" rather than a Lincolnesque virtue. The DSM-IV actually included DPD in one of its appendices as "worthy of further study," but the DSM-5 dropped all mention, and on a practical level it is not hard to see why: The DSM already has an entry called "dysthymia," which refers to a less severe depression that persists for at least two years. But could dysthymia in truth already be suggesting a depressive personality?

That is the way Hagop Akiskal, taking his lead from Kraepelin, employs the term.

Recall our discussion in "up" concerning "hypomania" and "hyperthymia," together with our example of Marilyn Monroe and your stereotypical librarian, both dancing on tables. Marilyn, we determined, was just being Marilyn. It was the librarian we needed to worry about.

Hypomania, you will recall, is the "state," hyperthymia the "trait." Viewed this way, Marilyn was acting well within her own personal sense of normal. Our librarian was not.

So, once more, let's imagine Marilyn and our librarian. Only, this time, instead of both dancing on tables, each one is home alone in bed, reading a book. Which one should we be worrying about now?

Marilyn vs the librarian. "Down" is relative. The top diagram above represents a classic case of Marilyn cycling into the uncomfortable low end of mild depression, perilously close to severe depression. On the bottom diagram representing our librarian, the cycling image is exactly the same. But check out the wider bandwidth. Her version of "normal" allows her a lot more clearance.

Looking at it this way, dysthymia is to a less severe form of depression as hyperthymia is to hypomania. This brings us back to my friend Therese and thinking deep. Therese is actually one of the funniest people I know. A sample from her 2010 book, *Beyond Blue*:

I have a magnet on my refrigerator that reads, "Jesus loves you, but everyone else thinks you're an asshole."

Or this ...

"Pretend that I am an editor with Ladies Home Journal," my therapist said. "I walk up to you and say, 'Hey, Therese! Good to see you. What have you been up to?' What will you say?

"Oh. Nothing much. Just hanging out in the community room of a psych ward with Allen, an eighty-five-year-old who has slept with

165

ninety-six women and wants to make it ninety-seven."

"*Try again,*" she said. "*You are still tutoring at the college, right?*"

"*Until the dean discovers a whackjob is teaching tomorrow's leaders.*"

I've always deployed humor in my writing, but it was Therese who urged me to bring it to the fore. Both of us, in so many respects, represent the archetype of the depressed clown. But then there are those demonstrably unfunny times.

Since the end of 2008, with the collapse of the financial markets, "persistent, loud, and maddening" death thoughts have haunted my friend. Nothing worked—not meds, not supplements, not meditation, not therapy, not rigorous physical exercise. She recounts one especially dark moment:

I felt as though I was trapped in between a brick wall and a pane of glass, like a jail cell that kept on shrinking, suffocating me as the space grew more confining. I wanted so badly out of life that I would have done just about anything to get there. Despite my Catholic faith and my strong religious beliefs, if a physician would have offered me some barbiturates to flatten my pulse, I don't think I would have hesitated to reach for them in desperation.

Then, five years into it, by the Severn River in Annapolis, she gave up. With that came a few moments of peace. Shortly after, she came across Holocaust survivor Viktor Frankl's *Man's Search for Meaning*.

This inspired her to take her efforts to a new level by launching a new Facebook support group, Group Beyond Blue, a new online community, Project Beyond Blue, and a nonprofit corporation, Beyond Blue Foundation.

According to Therese:

Dr Frankl's "logotherapy" is based on the belief that human nature is motivated by the search for a life purpose. If we devote our time and energy toward finding and pursuing the ultimate meaning of our life, we are able to transcend our suffering. It doesn't mean that we don't feel it. However, the meaning holds our hurt in a context that gives us peace. We must never forget that we may also find meaning in life even when confronted with a hopeless situation ...

Thinking deep is obviously part of Therese's "normal." Indeed, she recently informed me that she is learning to embrace her depression and accept that "what is—is what is."

Therese and son sharing a precious moment.

To complicate the matter, the two of us are also playful and experience our natural ups. Consider ourselves dividing our time between dysthymia and hyperthymia—

cyclothymic in the Kraepelin/Akiskal sense of the term. In a sense, we operate within a very wide bandwidth of "normal."

Perhaps we can look at our own versions of "normal" as where we feel safe, mildly depressed or not. But for others, mild depression may be too much to bear. Or a comfortable depression may morph into a suffocating one. When I first wrote about dysthymia back in 1999, I compared it to a form of Chinese water torture:

Day in and day out it grinds us down, robbing us of our will to succeed in life, to interact with others, and to enjoy the things that others take for granted. The gloom that is generated in our tortured brains spills outward into the space that surrounds us and warns away all those who might otherwise be our friends and associates and loved ones. All too frequently we find ourselves alone, shunned by the world around us and lacking the strength to make our presence felt.

You can find the above passage on my mcmanweb site and in my *Living Well* book, along with this ...

Still, we are able to function, a sort of death-in-life existence that gets us out into the world and to work and the duties of staying alive then back to our homes and the blessed relief of flopping into our unmade beds.

There's no way I could have written something like that if I hadn't personally experienced it—day in, day out, for weeks and months and years. Depression is still a constant in my life. What's different now for both Therese and me is that we the two of us found meaning in our lives. In 1999, when I began writing about my illness, suddenly my life had a purpose.

I know full well that Therese's life also had a purpose

long before her epiphany by the river. My guess is that her latest realization gave her a sense of renewal. We're fragile creatures. Meaning and purpose have expiration dates. Life grinds us down. Depression once more assumes the upper hand. In our distress, we lose our grip on the things that matter.

Paradoxically, this sets up the conditions for renewal and healing. This is when Therese gave up. This is when I, back in 1999, gave in to my despair. I've had to renew myself many times since then. The depression is always there, waiting to strike, to crush me, asphyxiate me, suck the life out of me.

Somehow, like Therese, I've learned to live with it, make it part of my "normal." Thinking deep is where I thrive, where I feel alive, even teetering on the edge of the abyss. But if I'm not careful, I can deep-think my way into an existential crisis. Next thing, I'm going to sleep hoping I never wake up.

Map of reality, close-up 15: As we zoom in on personality/ temperament, we see a more benign aspect of our depression we might describe as "thinking deep." But it may also take the form of pessimism or its more constructive variant, depressive realism. Finally, it may take on a more ominous aspect as a type of chronic malignancy that wears us down and sets us up for a major depression.

26. BREAKING DOWN DEPRESSION: AGITATED VS VEGETATIVE, PSYCHOTIC DEPRESSIONS, ANXIOUS DEPRESSIONS, SITUATIONAL VS CLINICAL

Why don't we be constructive and interpret the DSM symptom checklist in a way that might actually tell us something about depression? The first two symptoms, which form an either-or pair, actually provide an important key to the puzzle, namely:

EITHER feeling depressed most of the time for two weeks OR abnormal loss of interest or pleasure most of the time for two weeks.

One or the other has to be filled in. No checkmark, no depression.

Essentially, we are looking at a condition that involves either too much emotion (such as exaggerated sadness) or lack of emotion (such as manifest indifference to just about everything). Had the DSM highlighted this contrast, we would have the beginning of a credible dichotomy, one that suggests at least two different biological factors in play.

For instance, the serotonin system in the brain is most identified with mood while the dopamine system has to do with energy/arousal and anticipation/pleasure/reward. This is a gross oversimplification, mind you, but at least we're starting to separate the light from the dark. More on this in a minute ...

We also have a suite of three physical symptoms presented as opposites, Namely:

- Appetite or weight disturbance, either weight loss or weight gain.
- Sleep disturbance, either abnormal insomnia or abnormal hypersomnia.
- Activity (psychomotor) disturbance, either abnormal agitation or abnormal slowing (observable by others).

In addition, we have a fourth physical symptom expressed as abnormal fatigue or loss of energy.

Granted, these symptoms don't tell us what is going on inside our head, but they do represent fairly good markers of the brain in a state of distress. Obviously, someone who can't eat and sleep and is pacing about like an over-cranked wind-up toy is in very different mental shape than someone who can't stop eating and sleeping and can't move and lacks energy and motivation. Yet, it's easy to conceive of each state as a form of depression.

We also have three symptoms that probe for state of mind.

- Abnormal self-reproach or inappropriate guilt.
- Abnormal poor concentration or indecisiveness.
- Abnormal morbid thoughts of death (not just fear of dying) or suicide.

Unfortunately, these symptoms provide few clues into what may be going on beneath the hood: Stressed? Overwhelmed? Feeling empty?

Nor do we get a good read on our emotions: Blunted? Over-sensitive? Fearful? Not caring?

Nor do we get a sense of how we're thinking: Brain churning out a frenzy of scattered thoughts? Or stuck in the same dark thoughts? Or unable to put two thoughts together?

Still, even with these limited clues, it is easy to imagine two different states of mind. In the first, the affected individual is exhibiting outward signs of being an over-ruminating fearful nervous wreck. The other is showing little sign of life. Yet a doctor—with the full authority of psychiatry's diagnostic Bible—will diagnose each one with "depression" and send both out the door with the same prescription, namely an antidepressant.

By now, this far into this book, you are aware that an antidepressant is hardly a drug for all seasons, and needs to be prescribed with extreme caution. This was exactly the point Dr Koukopoulos made when I first heard him talk about agitated depression back in 2001.

By now, this far into this book, you are aware that an antidepressant is hardly a drug for all seasons, and needs to be prescribed with extreme caution. This was exactly the point Dr Koukopoulos made when I first heard him talk about agitated depression back in 2001.

The DSM does make an attempt to sort out depression "with melancholic features" from depression "with atypical features." In the diagnostic hierarchy, these are known as "specifiers," and due to their more lowly status they are easily overlooked.

Melancholy is regarded as an antiquated term for depression, but psychiatry sees it as a version of the second item in its first checklist pairing, namely involving loss of pleasure. In addition, melancholy is defined by marked psychomotor retardation and lack of reactivity to pleasurable stimuli. With atypical (which is actually fairly typical), on the other hand, reactivity is regarded the cardinal feature.

Thus, if you were to cheer up to news that you just won

the Powerball lottery, your depression would be regarded as "atypical." The catch is that the experts are now calling all this reactivity business into question. It simply doesn't hold up to close scrutiny. A little history …

Back in the sixties, researchers observed that certain patients responded better to a particular class of first-generation antidepressants—MAOIs such as Nardil—than another class—tricyclics such as imipramine. These responders fit the general profile of those with atypical features. As well as being reactive to events, they were also more likely to exhibit "hypersomnia" and "leaden paralysis."

In other words, there was an anergic or vegetative quality to these depressions. This would help explain why MAOIs, which give a slight boost to the dopamine system, proved so helpful. Any med that enhances dopamine firing is bound to act as an energizer, which is why cocaine and various forms of speed are popular drugs of abuse.

As a side issue, for many people a potent but safe energizer could be for many just what the doctor ordered, but that drug is currently just a gleam in some pharmacologist's eye. MAOIs, due to their onerous side effects, are now rarely prescribed. In the meantime, the advent of serotonin-enhancing antidepressants, such as Prozac and Paxil, have thrown researchers and clinicians off the dopamine scent.

There may be many valid reasons for distinguishing between melancholic and atypical depression, but that particular conversation distracts us from consideration of what has to be the prominent depression divide—agitated (energized) and vegetative (retarded) depressions. Thus:

Agitated depressions: Energy surges, wound up, too much emotion, under-eating, little sleep, over-thinking, over-rumination.

Vegetative depressions: Low energy and fatigue, loss of pleasure, low motivation, little emotion, over-eating, sluggish thinking.

As a thought experiment, you might want to ask yourself how feelings of sadness or guilt fit into this dichotomy. Could you be too agitated, for instance to feel sad or guilty? Or could you lack the energy to produce such emotions?

Complicating the issue is the fact that men express their emotions much differently than women. This is the point I raised with Robert Spitzer at our chance dinner together back in 2003. You know how that went over. More on this in the next chapter.

Further complicating the issue is psychosis. According to a 2001 sample of a large population, one in five patients with depression experience psychotic features in their depressions. These tend to take the form of "mood-congruent" delusions, such as the false impression that one deserves to be in hell.

Recall the psychosis Maricela experienced when she was manic, how she thought she was in the company of angels. With depression, mood-congruency goes in the other direction. Thus, if we are already experiencing hell, it is not difficult for our already deluded brains to come up with the lighting and the staging. As with mania, the psychosis goes away when the episode goes away.

Far more common is anxiety. In 2013, the DSM-5 introduced "with anxious distress" as a specifier to major depression. This loosely corresponds to the neurosis-driven depressions of the ancient DSMs I and II, which—contrary to conventional wisdom—do a fairly good job in giving us a feel for the sheer complexity of "down."

Say, for instance, you have just been downsized. Not

only will you feel depressed, but you will be expressing extreme worry and anxiety over paying your bills and surviving. The DSM mentions feeling "keyed up and tense," "unusually restless," having "difficulty concentrating because of worry," being fearful "that something awful may happen," and feeling one "might lose control."

It is perfectly normal, of course, to feel devastated and lost when life overtakes you. This best describes "situational" depression, and we can also apply it to bereavement. The understanding is that you will return to normal once life returns to normal.

But suppose your depression persists? Situational turns "clinical." Your depression, in effect, has taken on a life of its own, and this is where the illness assumes a new level of double-whammy cruelty. For instance, if you have just lost your job, you need your wits about you to regroup, take charge, and search for other employment. Not only do you need to be on your full cognitive and social game, you need the emotional wherewithal to bounce back from one inevitable disappointment to the next.

What is depression going to do to that?

Walk into any support group and you will hear stories of how people never recovered once their economic security was yanked out from under them. This is one reason the World Health Organization ranks depression as the second leading cause of disability, worldwide, after lower respiratory diseases. (Bipolar is number six.) It's not the kill rate. It's the fact that in contrast to, say, heart disease, depression tends to strike at a fairly early age and take us out of the game, when we are in our prime.

Just so we're clear—depression doesn't need a valid reason to live inside your brain. A stupid reason or no reason at all works just fine. What we need to know is that we possess vulnerable brains sensitive to the slightest shifts in our environment, be it a relationship going sour, recollection of past trauma, or a change in the seasons.

Finally, we need to be aware that with bipolar nothing ever stands still. We may pat ourselves on the back for dividing depression into agitated and vegetative, only to discover that nature has spun the wheel—cycles, cycles—and turned our brains upside down and its contents into a hopeless jumble.

What may be a magic bullet for unipolar may turn out to be a poison pill for bipolar. We may have cleared up the symptom of the day only to discover, to our horror, that we have accelerated all those wheels within wheels.

No one ever said this was going to be easy.

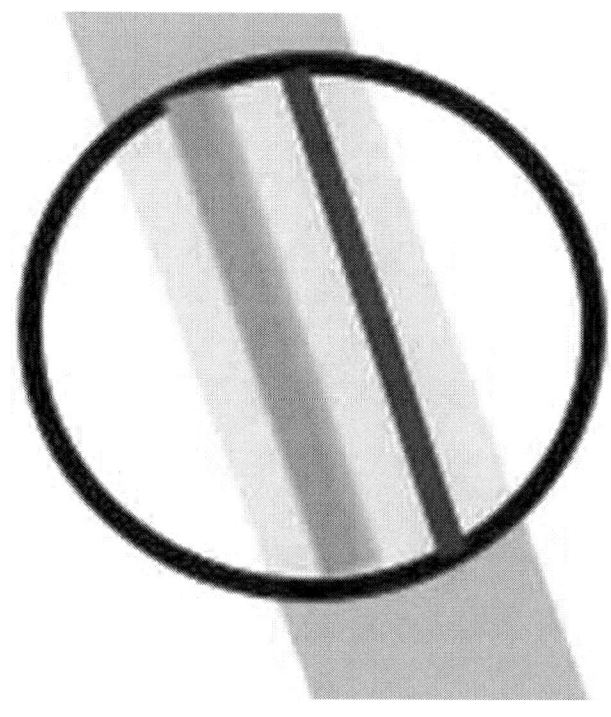

Map of reality, close-up 16: If we must simplify depression, it is probably most instructive to see it as taking two distinct forms. When we zoom in, we see an agitated or energized depression (represented by the thicker line) and a vegetative or retarded depression (represented by the thin dark line). Unipolar depressions tend to manifest more as agitated depressions, but you never know.

27. BREAKING DOWN BIPOLAR DEPRESSION

In *Living Well with Depression and Bipolar Disorder*, I briefly described my first psychiatric visit. I was in a state of suicidal depression. All I could talk about were my depressions, all of them, namely:

My depression within a depression, my depression following the depression on top of the depression, and so on. My "ups" were what I mistook for normal behavior, so I did not feel compelled to bring them to my psychiatrist's attention. Besides, considering the state I was in, he wasn't about to mistake me for the type who danced on tables.

I did suggest to my psychiatrist, not all that convincingly, that I might have this thing called manic-depression or bipolar or whatever. But that would have required a specific example or two, such as the time twelve years before when I flipped out and became unemployable. But it never entered my mind to bring this up.

And none of those people from way back who knew I had to be totally bonkers were there to prompt me.

Also, I had no knowledge then of the skeletons in my family closet, including a grandfather who required electro-convulsive therapy. My grandfather, incidentally, once threw a chessboard up in the air after my younger six-year-old brother checkmated him. In my family, they referred to this type of behavior as normal.

As for my father—I later learned from my mother that he had secretly sought therapy for depression. He paid for these visits out of his own pocket, such was his fear of being found out and fired from his office job. Looking back, he probably would have fallen on the low end of the bipolar spectrum. Back in those days—the early sixties—antidepressant treatment was fairly rare. Otherwise, on such medication, he might have flipped into mania, lost his job, and left us destitute.

In other words, my family was genetically loaded with bipolar, but who knew?

Thus, in the absence of convincing evidence, my psychiatrist decided I had unipolar depression and prescribed an antidepressant. Within a couple of days, I was feeling good. Better than good, in fact. Super good, full of energy. I started making plans, grand plans. My heart was racing, I couldn't sleep. Wait! Are luminous and vaguely animal-shaped objects supposed to be hovering just below the ceiling?

Time to take my next pill.

Perhaps you can appreciate my dilemma. Three days before, I was clinging for dear life just above the abyss, about to let go. Now here I was, significantly disengaged from rational thinking, floating in the lower atmosphere with unidentified flying objects. Do I take that pill and risk becoming lost in space? Or forego the medicine and face the prospect of a precipitous free-fall back into the abyss?

Fortunately, I had the presence of mind to skip my dose and leave a message with my psychiatrist. I was referred to a crisis intervention team. Babbling a mile-a-minute before three women—one who I was convinced had developed an instant crush on me—made my diagnosis a no-brainer.

Soon, I was on the right meds and my condition stabilized. I was a long way from feeling great, but at least I was no longer suicidally depressed. Ironically, bad psychiatry probably saved my life. That antidepressant literally launched me out of the gravitational field of my Dante-proportioned personal hell. Granted, I overshot normal by a light-year or two, but in the grand scheme of things I choose to refer to that as a temporary side effect.

Of all things, I couldn't have asked for a better outcome.

Suppose, for instance, my antidepressant had acted closer to expectations. In this scenario, it would have taken three or four weeks for a slight improvement to manifest. Could I have held on that long? And assuming I did hold on and my mood lifted to the point where I could begin to see light at the end of the tunnel, how long would that have lasted before mental agitation set in or the drug eventually pooped out?

But that modest improvement would have only encouraged any psychiatrist. Standard procedure when the first antidepressant doesn't work or is badly tolerated is to try another. Then another. As we learned earlier, this tends to go on for years. Eventually, a psychiatrist—perhaps my fifth or sixth by then—would have put two and two together and made the right diagnostic call, but how manageable would my bipolar be, after years of my neurons being bombarded by the wrong drugs?

This is the point Robert Whittaker makes in his 2010 book, *Anatomy of an Epidemic*. This view, with strong reservations, is entirely consistent with those espoused by Drs Goodwin and Ghaemi. I will be going into this in much greater depth in a future book on treatment. For now, we simply need to recognize that I was delivered from all this by my propitious over-reaction.

But were there other signs—less tell-tale, to be sure—my psychiatrist should have been paying attention to?

In earlier chapters, I stressed the importance of

searching for evidence of previous depressions. Basically—and this bears constant repetition—we need to think of bipolar as a cycling illness characterized by recurring depressions separated by "up."

Never mind how high up has to be. It's simply enough knowing that up is suggested by those past depressions. I would submit that when in doubt, our doctors should err on the side of diagnosing bipolar rather than depression, that bipolar should be the default diagnosis.

It's fairly obvious that doctors use stigma concerns as their diagnostic tie-breaker. I submit that the risk of harm from antidepressants renders stigma insignificant, by comparison. I cannot repeat this enough: Antidepressants and bipolar do not mix.

Okay, here's the question: Could my psychiatrist have found bipolar clues in my CURRENT depression? Yes and no. I do recall telling my psychiatrist how agitated I felt. At the time, I knew nothing of agitated depressions or how such conditions could even be possible.

Agitated depressions, of course, are one of the hallmarks of a bipolar mixed state. But this was 1999, when psychiatry assumed mixed states were a rarity.

My agitation also could have pointed to the type of depressions men more commonly experience. The male species, you will recall, express their emotions differently than women. When we get depressed, we tend to show it by getting angry rather than weepy, and by being antisocial and aggressive rather than expressing guilt and anguish. Moreover, we don't exactly initiate heart-to-hearts with the boys. On top of that, when we run to the fridge, it's not for the Ben and Jerry's. Finally, we're far less likely to display the type of suicidal behavior that raises alarm bells with those close to us.

Basically, men are from Testosterone, women from

Estrogen. Neurotransmitters such as serotonin and dopamine may get all the attention, but our hormones are every bit as influential on our moods, if not more so. Certainly, they shape our depressions.

I will be going into this in far greater detail in future books. For the time being, what you need to know is that my psychiatrist was looking at a man about to hit the mid-century mark, apparently defeated by life, and not hiding his sense of anger and frustration. My agitation was clearly sending up a red flag. When this happens, Dr Koukopolos told us in Pittsburgh in 2001, the clinician's priority is to calm down the patient. The doctor's first option, in other words, should not necessarily involve writing a prescription for an antidepressant.

Just to totally confuse you, those with bipolar depression tend to exhibit vegetative qualities rather than agitated. This includes such features as motor retardation, more time sleeping, and weight gain. In an article in *Psychiatric Services* in 2001, Charles Bowden of the University of Texas, San Antonio also pointed to acute onset or abatement of symptoms, and greater lability (ie more instability such as mood swings) during episodes.

Dr Bowden's article represents a consensus among researchers into bipolar depression, so let's continue. The article also mentioned that those with bipolar depression tend to have much higher scores for extraversion, novelty-seeking, and being less judgmental than their unipolar counterparts.

Dr Bowden also brought up seasonal depression, which is more likely to manifest in those in the bipolar spectrum. The DSM recognizes "seasonal affective disorder" characterized by depressions believed to result from winter reductions in natural light. Recall our particular vulnerability to even the slightest cyclical fluctuations, including the seasons.

We also have age of onset. As a general rule, bipolar tends to turn up at an earlier age than unipolar depression. Typically, this occurs during the transition from youth to adult, in the late-teens and early twenties. But here is the catch: Those first episodes are inevitably depressive ones. The mania outbreaks tend to occur later.

Having pointed out these clues (together with evidence of past depressions), Dr Bowden cautioned that "no single or specific constellation of these symptomatic presentations allows unequivocal diagnosis of unipolar or bipolar depression."

This lets my first psychiatrist off the hook. Actually, he proved his worth many times over in later visits. Here, he displayed great concern for my welfare and was extremely supportive in my launching a new career as a mental health journalist. Most of all, I shall be eternally grateful that he kept my mood stabilizer at a low dose, much lower than the ones most bipolar patients are put on. This, I'm convinced, freed me to begin my recovery.

Nevertheless, looking back on that fateful evening when I was bouncing off the walls and ceilings, I cannot help but wonder: Had I taken that antidepressant when I was supposed to, where would I be now?

Map of reality, close-up 17: In this zoom-in view of bipolar depression, we see vegetative depression as the more common form. But don't be fooled. Our tendency to transition to hypomania and mania may produce mixed states that result in a good deal of agitation.

28. REVIEWING "DOWN"

In 2014, in a blog piece on *HealthCentral*, I asked my readers: If you had access to a magic pill that could cure you of your bipolar right now, forever, would you take it?

The answer was an unambiguous hell yes.

I can certainly identify with this response. There is no way to describe the hells I've endured with this illness. And heaven forbid, should another killer depression come along.

But I would have to answer no. Certainly not a hell no. But a no just the same. It all has to do with who I am. Or who I think I am.

Conventional psychiatry regards bipolar as an outside force that has nothing to do with who we really are. Eradicate the bipolar like a virus, in other words, and at last we can experience our lives as normal people do. But as we know by now, personality and illness are inextricably linked. Each is embedded in the other. Like it or not, my bipolar informs my sense of self, who I really am.

So, if a magic pill could remove my bipolar, what else would it remove? Would my bipolar "cure" amount to a personality amputation? As I wrote on *HealthCentral*:

People have died in battle, been burned at the stake, been shipped off to the death camps, refusing—to their last heroic breath—to yield their sense of identity. Am I willing to let go of mine so readily, even in the name of a cure?

Do I really want to wake up—a different person?

I went on to say that if we are so quick to blame bipolar

186

for everything wrong about us, can we not at least give the illness credit for a few things that might be right with us? Our creativity, for one? Our deep thinking, for another?

If nothing else, I wrote, can we not give our illness grudging acknowledgement for the highly complex, multi-dimensional beings we turned out to be? I have no doubt that life without bipolar would be a lot easier and more pain-free for me. But at what cost? What cost?

This concludes Part IV on mapping down. To summarize:

- Mania and hypomania get most of the attention, but we actually spend far more of our time being depressed. Not only that, depression is more disabling and lethal than mania or hypomania.
- Depression should not be considered one illness with a single cause. More likely, we're looking at a number of different illnesses that bear the same name. One consequence of a simplistic depression mindset is that one-size-fits-all treatments and therapies work well for only some.
- Psychiatry distinguishes between chronic depression and recurrent depression. As a rough guide, a chronic course would be regarded as unipolar while highly recurrent depressions would fall within the bipolar spectrum.
- Even the experts are in the dark concerning depression's myriad expressions and underlying causes. Stress and trauma, personal loss, sensitivity to the seasons, and gender are just some of the many factors that come into play.
- Nevertheless, it is safe to say that depression is part of a dynamic that involves our biology and environment acting on each other. In short, our

187

vulnerable brains have a difficult time adjusting to our surroundings.

- Psychiatry has attempted to separate depression into melancholic and atypical. A more useful separation, I submit, would be agitated and vegetative. Having said that, with bipolar, nothing ever stands still.
- Anxiety also looms large in depression.
- We also need to pay regard to situational vs clinical depressions, and how the former could morph into the latter.
- Bipolar depressions may have different clinical features than unipolar depressions, but these features are merely suggestive rather than definitive.
- Finally, we need to have regard for the fact that many of us have depressive temperaments distinct from but related to our depressive episodes. For many of us, then, mild chronic depression—dysthymia—may be part of our true normal.
- Living within our true normal may involve cultivating a sense of acceptance, but that is not the same as giving up. The trick is to find a certain level of comfort within ourselves without allowing ourselves to become overwhelmed by our depressive tendencies.

Let's move on to "normal" ...

PART FIVE: MAPPING "NORMAL"

What piece of work is a man!

— Shakespeare, Hamlet

29. IS CRAZY YOUR TRUE NORMAL? CREATIVITY, GENIUS, AND LEADERSHIP

In his 2011 book, *A First-Rate Madness*, Nassir Ghaemi describes a quest by one of Freud's last disciples, Roy Grinker. This involved a search for "normal."

In pursuit of his goal, Dr Grinker screened a group of 343 college-age men, out of which he selected 65 he deemed to be in the middle of the mentally healthy range. Based on subsequent interviews, Grinker came up with a detailed list of mental health attributes for these "upright young men."

There was, however, a major catch. These paragons of mental health suffered a severe case of "average-itis." They had slightly above average IQs, their grades were average, and they were not leaders on the team sports they had played in high school.

About the best you could say of them was they played well with others. Dr Grinker came up with the term "homoclite" to describe these drearily normal individuals —"those who follow a common rule." Their goals were to fit in, do good, and be liked. Apparently they would grow up to become part of the "great silent majority" that Nixon so infamously pandered to.

As Dr Ghaemi points out in his book, Dr Grinker's homoclites represented the norm (a statistical average) and normal (an absence of illness), but hardly an ideal. Basically, Dr Ghaemi is validating what many of us have known all along—that normal is highly overrated.

Maybe, then, "different" is good. At my 2010 talk to the Kansas State DBSA conference, someone asked me about famous people with mental illness. Here was my answer:

We discovered fire. I don't care if nobody wrote this down. Anyone crazy enough to go out into a burning forest and bring a flaming twig back inside a cave was not normal, was not thinking linearly, okay?

And just everything, from discovering America to painting the Sistine Chapel to writing Beethoven's Ninth to great poetry, great works of literature, to Isaac Newton, great works of science. I mean, literally, every field of human endeavor, we brought the world the gift of civilization and how does society treat us? We get marginalized.

I was obviously on fire that day, but before we assign credit exclusively to depression and mania, let's give recognition to our true normal. "Here's to the crazy ones," opens the iconic 1997 Apple TV ad. "The misfits. The rebels. The troublemakers. The round pegs in the square holes. The ones who see things differently … "

These different people included the likes of Einstein, Dylan, Amelia Earhart, Gandhi, Picasso, Maria Callas, Ted Turner, Martin Luther King, and so on. These are clearly not Grinker's homoclites. But before we pat ourselves on the back for being different, they are hardly your classic bipolar cases, either.

Here's the deal: When I'm going through a bear of a depression, I lack the will to get out of bed, much less write the great post-modernist American novel. When manicky or anxious, my mind is far too unsettled for the seat of my pants to make a date with the seat of my chair. The good news is that when my brain does settle down or my depression lifts I don't magically turn into a Grinker homoclite.

Most of this, no doubt, has to do with personality traits totally unrelated to bipolar. But it is important to note that my depressive and manicky symptoms don't entirely shut down, either, when I reenter my comfort zone. I'm still thinking deep and my thoughts are still racing full blast. That's one reason I'm able to write this book.

Perhaps it is fair to say, then, that crazy is my true normal. But the catch is not straying too far outside of it.

Okay, let's examine the one individual in the Apple line-up we know to have been diagnosed with bipolar, the swashbuckling businessman Ted Turner, the "mouth from the south" who created CNN and Turner Broadcasting. In his book, Dr Ghaemi contends that Turner was a success because of, rather than despite, his bipolar. But the bipolar gods may have been kinder to Turner than to us. The course of his illness, Ghaemi points out, was constant rather than episodic.

To freely interpret, state and trait appeared to have blended seamlessly, allowing long periods of certainty— dare I say normal?—in his life. This is a massively different proposition than lurching unpredictably from one productive hypomania to the next, with who knows what in between.

Dr Ghaemi ascribes a good deal of Turner's success to his "manic creativity," his preternatural knack for anticipating trends and opportunities—not to mention problems—and hitting upon novel courses of action. According to Ghaemi, Turner saw himself as a "divergent thinker."

In divergent thinking, the brain essentially free-ranges across a vast landscape of disparate thoughts and perceptions, taking in everything, ruling out nothing. This roughly corresponds to the "flight of ideas" symptom in mania. When joined with a problem needing to be solved (which creative people tend to go looking for), the apparent randomness of the exercise may turn serendipitous. Just ask Einstein.

Leading neuropsychiatrist Nancy Andreasen of the University of Iowa speculates that in creative people, the brain's association cortices may facilitate the connection of two or more apparently unrelated items into that mind-boggling Eureka! moment. As she told a packed room at the 2007 American Psychiatric Association annual meeting in San Diego: "In a way, the brain disorganizes to self-organize to produce a new idea."

Dr Andreasen's initial investigations into creativity centered on a possible schizophrenia connection. Einstein, she said, exhibited schizotypal tendencies, a form of schizophrenia lite. This brings us to some new ways of looking at "low latent inhibition" (LLI). LLI relates to the brain's difficulty in tuning out stimuli in the environment. One result is that the brain treats the familiar as novel.

The phenomenon is identified with psychosis and schizophrenia, and to a lesser extent with bipolar. It is also becoming a hot new research field in creativity.

If LLI sounds a lot like divergent thinking to you, you may be correct. It could be that in certain respects the creative brain and the bipolar brain are similarly organized (perhaps disorganized is the more appropriate term). This would explain in part why a disease that the World Health Organization ranks sixth in terms of disability also accounts for a wildly disproportionate share of artists and literary figures and musicians and composers.

But it hardly explains the roster of high achievers in the Apple commercial. In addition to the people already listed, the footage includes John Lennon, Richard Branson, Bucky Fuller, Edison, Muhammad Ali, Alfred Hitchcock, Martha Graham, Frank Lloyd Wright, and Jim Henson. To a person, these luminaries were (and some still are) masters of divergent thinking. But what else did they have—that we don't?

The answer could be "executive function." This has to do with the ability of the cortical areas of the brain to make sense of what is going on in real time and to regulate our behavior accordingly. Executive function has been described as the CEO of the brain. More like a chief operating officer (COO), I would say, but let's not quibble.

Those with schizophrenia face major challenges in this department. So, to a lesser extent, do many of us with bipolar, even when not symptomatic. In cognitive tests involving solving mind puzzles with the clock ticking, non-episodic individuals with bipolar fared worse than the control subjects. These same studies also revealed that the cortical regions in our brain must work harder to process even routine tasks.

This may be fine when things are going right. But turn up the heat or introduce stress into the equation and our capacity to deal with life in real time becomes severely compromised.

This is exactly what happened to me in the meeting I described in Chapter Two. Too much going on in my mind combined with one too many aggressively stupid people. I literally felt my brain overloading, unable to make sense of the situation and access the neural networks I needed to form coherent responses.

This wasn't about depression or mania. Basically, my own "normal" failed me. Had the heat been turned up a degree or two more, my fight or flight response might have kicked in. In these situations, the thinking parts of the brain cede dominion to the reactive parts. Fortunately, I managed to hold myself together and exit the meeting in one piece without making a scene.

Just so there is no misunderstanding: I wasn't a powder keg ready to explode. Very much the opposite.

We also need to emphasize that in many situations the person with bipolar may be the only calm one in the room. It works like this: When life deviates from the script, the chronically normal tend to find themselves at a loss. This is much the point of Dr Ghaemi's book. Normal brains, which were built for normal times, tend to prove inadequate in times of crisis. Reason fails them. They make bad decisions.

By contrast, the individual with the freakish ability to see around corners may prove the man or woman of the hour. Dr Ghaemi cites numerous historical examples, most famously the raging depressive Winston Churchill during the Second World War.

Having said that, however, we also need to acknowledge how our vulnerabilities also have a way of reducing us to nothing. Even just being thrown off our game a little bit can have devastating consequences. Too often, it's the seemingly inconsequential things that undermine our ability to be at the top of our game: The thrum of the air-conditioner that we are unable to tune out, the sun suddenly appearing through a slit in the blinds.

Heaven help if we have to keep track of two conversations at once or recall our PIN number on a crowded street corner in a strange city. It's as if, when we're not looking, someone is rearranging things inside our brain, shuffling papers, moving furniture, turning out lights.

Trust me, to the world-changing people in the Apple commercial, such intrusions are minor distractions at best. Thus, thanks to being firmly grounded in the rational world, they and people like them are able to stay on task and reap the full benefits of crazy.

Crazy, huh?

On a final note, a 2011 study conducted on a large Swedish population found a correlation between bipolar and creativity that was higher than among the general population. But the real beneficiaries were the first-degree relatives, who possessed similar talents without contending with the downsides of a chronic mental disorder. These were the people, apparently, who hit the genetic jackpot— north of normal, south of bipolar.

If only, if only. But let's be grateful for what we've got. Yes, we all long for a quiet life in normal, but on reflection, is that what we really want?

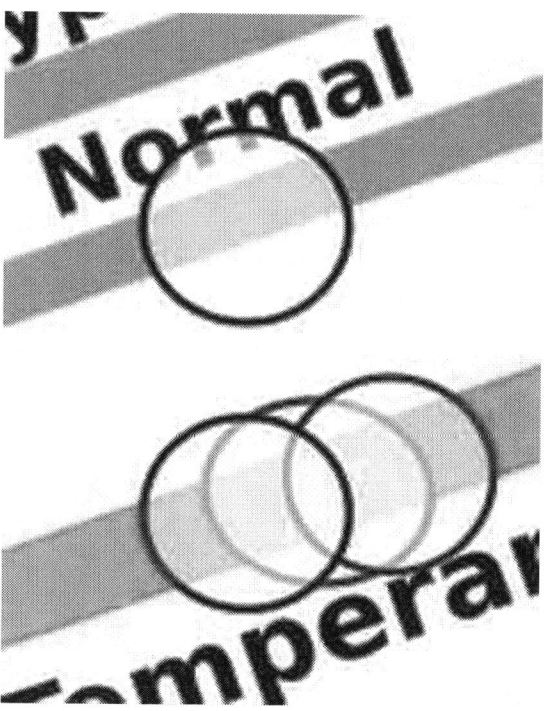

Map of reality, close-up 18: Different perspectives of "normal." In the upper line, we see "normal" as that lucid interval between mood episodes, though we may still be buffeted about by depression and mania and anxiety. "Normal" also varies from individual to individual. Some people have a much wider safety clearance in their cycles than others.

The three overlapping circles along personality/temperament represent different aspects of our so-called "true" normal, namely: 1) Grinker's "homoclites" representing an average or norm, but hardly an ideal. 2) Positive character traits such as creativity and leadership representing something closer to an ideal. 3) Negative character traits such as impulsivity or hostility pointing to what is holding us back. Our personalities represent a blend of all three realms, but some of us exhibit a more enviable combination than others.

Finally, we need to have regard for the fact that mood and personality hardly exist in isolation. Each influences the other.

30. WHEN "NORMAL" GOES WRONG: BORDERLINE PERSONALITY DISORDER

In 2005, back when I was active in a local DBSA in New Jersey, I joined the board of a state DBSA we were trying to form. There, I came across behavior from hell—extremely abusive verbal attacks, explosive meltdowns, public outbursts, poison pen emails, delusional self-centeredness, love and light one minute, fire and brimstone the next.

For my own self-preservation, I got the hell out. Was this bipolar? Or was it something else? Borderline personality disorder? I needed to find out. The first stop in my journey was the 2006 APA annual meeting in Toronto. Unexpectedly, the first borderline discussion there occurred during question time at a packed luncheon symposium on bipolar II.

Drs Goodwin, Akiskal, and Ghaemi were the featured speakers, along with Terrence Ketter of Stanford. I showed up early to make sure I got a good seat. Dr Ketter said that as opposed to bipolar disorder, which is about MOOD lability (volatility), borderline personality disorder is about EMOTIONAL lability. As soon as they develop an emotion stabilizer (analogous to a mood stabilizer), he said, borderline personality disorder would become an Axis I disorder rather than Axis II.

A little history: The DSM-III of 1980 introduced the axis system to mental disorders (since done away with in 2013 by the DSM-5). In general, illnesses that could be treated by meds (that by implication had a biological component) were assigned Axis I status. The personality disorders, including borderline, were lumped into Axis II. As biological psychiatry gained in influence, Axis II came to be seen as the last refuge of Freud.

What Dr Ketter was saying, in a diplomatic way, was that borderline had a way to go before it picked up respect.

Dr Ghaemi referred to borderline as a "clinical condition" rather than a disease, one best treated by psychotherapy. In a 2013 journal article, he fully elaborated. The DSM-III, he wrote, erred mightily when it classified all its diagnostic entries as "disorders," as if bipolar were not to be taken seriously as a medical illness.

Basically, bipolar is from Kraepelin, borderline from Freud. Two different world views, but could there be a reconciliation?

Dr Goodwin, who was running the proceedings, turned to Dr Akiskal, and in a friendly way goaded him: "Come now," he said, "what do you do with the patients you don't like?" Words to that effect.

Nothing could have prepared me for what came next. "I like all my patients!" Dr Akiskal thundered. Then: "I don't have any use for the borderline diagnosis."

Hold off on that reconciliation.

It didn't take me long to discover that Dr Akiskal had been waging war against borderline for decades. A 1985 article he co-authored had this title: "Borderline: An Adjective in Search of a Noun."

The next day found me in a largely vacant hall listening to Joel Paris of McGill University deliver an award lecture on personality disorders. Significantly, he was not about to let Dr Akiskal go unanswered. Referring to Dr Akiskal's long-standing hostility to borderline, Dr Paris let it be known, "I would say that is wrong."

In true Axis I depression, Dr Paris explained, when

patients come out of a depression, they are nice people again. Individuals with personality disorders, by contrast, can come out of a depression and still have problems with life. Unfortunately, clinicians prefer not to want to hear about personality. It means trouble. They would rather throw more meds at the problem.

In the five years I had been attending APA meetings to that point, you would scarcely know there was such a thing as personality disorders. But that would change three years hence. The 2009 APA annual meeting in San Francisco had nearly as many presentations devoted to personality disorders and related issues as to mood disorders. Moreover, its experts were speaking to packed rooms. A major sea change had occurred. Personality disorders were gaining respect.

Perhaps "regaining" is the more appropriate term. Recall that for the longest time Freud and his followers ruled the roost, typically to the detriment of serious scientific enquiry. How bad was it?

At the 2004 APA meeting in New York, I heard Jack Barchas, the man who identified serotonin's connection to behavior, recall way back having his ideas challenged by his mentor. "How is this justified in the writings of Freud?" asked the mentor.

Science, you will recall, advances one funeral at a time.

But bipolar hardly explained the appalling behavior I had encountered while   trying to set up a state DBSA. Had psychiatry, in effect, failed them? Sent them out the door with the wrong diagnosis and useless meds and false hopes? By 2009, if the APA meeting that year were anything to go by, the rank and file in psychiatry appeared to be asking similar questions.

Why, in effect, weren't their bipolar patients getting better? Was there a missing piece to the puzzle?

201

At first blush, borderline appears very much like bipolar disorder, and the DSM symptom list does little to disabuse us of that notion. Thus, borderline symptoms 4 through 7: impulsivity, recurrent suicidal behavior, affective instability, chronic feelings of emptiness.

In addition, borderline includes a symptom that one could, with reservations, apply to bipolar mixed states: "Inappropriate or intense anger or difficulty controlling anger."

In a 2006 article in the *American Journal of Psychiatry*, John Gunderson of Harvard noted that misdiagnosing patients with bipolar, especially bipolar II, is the norm. According to Dr Gunderson, periods of depression and irritability are rarely instructive. Neither are sustained periods of elation. What we are really looking for are reactions to interpersonal stress.

This harkens back to the days of the "maladaptions" of the ancient DSMs I and II, only this time we have support from modern brain science. In 2008, the NIMH reported on a series of brain imaging studies led by Michael Minzenberg of the University of California, Davis. In one study, in response to being shown images of "scary faces" (a common research practice), patients diagnosed with borderline displayed overactivity in the amygdala (involved in fight or flight) and underactivity in the anterior cingulate cortex (which acts as a modulator to limbic over-excitement.)

Once more we have a classic picture of the thinking parts of the brain being overwhelmed by the reactive parts of the brain. This is a scenario that cuts across a host of psychiatric conditions and blurs their distinctions. The study hardly constitutes proof of the borderline diagnosis. But clearly, we are looking at brains not optimally equipped to handle life.

The money question, then, is what is unique about borderline? The answer lies in those "maladaptions." The best-known involves "splitting," in which people are perceived as either all good or all bad, nothing in between. In DSM-speak, we see "a pattern of unstable and intense interpersonal relationships characterized by alternating between extremes of idealization and devaluation."

"Splitting" extends to manipulative behavior, in which the "all-good" individual receives favor at the expense of the "all-bad" one. That is, until the all-good party becomes all-bad. This can happen in the blink of an eye. Suddenly, for no apparent reason, the party with borderline lets loose on his or her victim, erupts, explodes.

Or it may be more subtle—the silent treatment, inappropriate put-downs. If the borderline party is nursing some kind of resentment, this can go on forever. Those living around someone with borderline compare the experience to walking on eggshells.

But would you want to trade places with such an individual? Throw in other DSM symptoms such as fear of abandonment, identity disturbance, and stress-induced paranoia, and a portrait emerges of an extremely fragile individual negotiating a frightening and unpredictable world, at a loss how to respond. Marsha Linehan of the University of Washington, who devised dialectical behavioral therapy (DBT) as a means to help her patients navigate their terrifying environment, says "borderline patients are the psychological equivalent of a third-degree burn patient."

I received an insight into this during the next stage of my journey, at the 2006 NAMI convention in Washington DC. Significantly, NAMI had just expanded its list of "priority populations" to include those with borderline personality disorder. This meant, probably for the first time, their convention had a session devoted to the illness. There, I had a chance to listen to patients speaking openly in an environment where they felt safe.

"Anne," in her late 30s-early 40s, came across as someone who had it all— smart, attractive, personable. She had a degree in creative writing, but the best job she could get was answering phones. Her illness cannot take the demands of something more challenging, she informed us. Amongst people, in stressful situations, she loses it. You don't want to be around her.

As opposed to walking on eggshells, Anne compared her dealings with people to "walking on shifting boards." The world is far from a safe place, she related, and the ground beneath her could collapse any second.

"It's like demons possess me," she went on to say. Something inside of yourself so overwhelms you that you want to change it instantly. Such as slitting your wrists, impulsive sex, alcohol, and acting out. She described individuals with borderline as spontaneous and lively and loving until they get hurt. Then they screw up and fall apart.

So—does Anne come across as a different breed of human than you? Consider:

Conventional psychiatry regards bipolar as episodic. This strongly suggests that our depressions and hypomanias and manias and anxieties bear primary responsibility for our extreme and often outrageous behaviors. The implication is that once we settle down to normal we feel mortified and ashamed by the actions of our evil twin. Hopefully, as our "real selves," we can return to our old lives of being model citizens and ideal partners and all the rest.

With personality disorders, however, there are no episodes, no evil twins. Life is played out in normal, and normal is booby-trapped with situations that constantly go wrong. If there happen to be additional concerns such as being caught up in one's delusional sense of self-importance or lacking any capacity for empathy, there may be no remorse, no regrets.

In personality disorders, in other words, there is no safe harbor, no place to call home. "Normal" is a dangerous location, a permanent hell. Once I grasped this, all the pieces fell into place. Not only did it explain the abominable natures of the people I ran into trying to set up a state DBSA, it also filled in the blanks on all those miserable people in my life who had been sent to earth for the sole purpose of testing me.

Thank God I'm not one of them, was my first reaction. I may be crazy, but at least I'm not an asshole.

Not so fast …

31. RECONCILING MOOD AND PERSONALITY

Personality does not yield to ready analysis, and heaven help if it ever did. For years, the DSM's Axis II section, where personality disorders used to reside, was by far its most problematic. It's not that the old-timers in the field didn't know what they were doing. To the contrary, their powers of clinical observation rivaled Kraepelin's.

It's just that organizing our destructive behaviors into neat symptom lists is simply asking too much. For instance, is someone who abruptly breaks off a friendship an "antisocial" individual with no remorse or a person with "borderline" who can't cope? Perhaps your classic "narcissist" who cares only about him or herself?

The DSM-5 work group charged with updating personality disorders expressly recognized the limits of symptom lists when they proposed a parallel "dimensional" system to sit alongside a reformed "categorical" one. On one level, this would have allowed clinicians and their patients to effectively build their own diagnosis, much like IKEA furniture, based on interchangeable parts. On another, even using the old labels, the casual reader would have picked up an appreciation for how common personality traits (such as hostility and impulsivity) cut across numerous categorical lines and blur them.

In the end, institutional opposition proved too strong. The old symptom lists stayed, along with their impermeable categorical walls. A chopped-down version of the working group's proposals was consigned to the back of the DSM-5 under the heading, "Alternative

Model for Personality Disorders."

Now that we've set the scene, we need to bring Dr Akiskal back into the picture. As you recall, Dr Akiskal has gone on record for his contempt of the borderline diagnosis, a position that placed him in the mainstream back in 1985 but has left him pretty much on his own in the second decade of this millennium. And, if you think categorically—bipolar symptom list vs borderline symptom list—it's easy to see why.

But Dr Akiskal has been a dimensional thinker all his life, and this changes everything. In the dimensional world, dueling symptom lists are a distraction. Instead, we are looking to achieve a synthesis, but on a much larger scale, some kind of grand theory of practically everything. Here, Dr Akiskal puts his money where his mouth is.

In two articles in the *Journal of Affective Disorders* in 2006, with the Brazilian Diogo Lara as his main collaborator, he published what I refer to as his "fear and anger equation." In a nutshell, Akiskal and Lara work from these two basic emotions to embrace nearly the entire universe of mood and temperament. The authors take an expansive view of anger to include a "sunny side." Thus, high anger and low fear brackets hyperthymia while reversing the highs and lows embraces depression.

Drs Akiskal and Lara point out that their model also applies to behavioral characteristics not associated with mood disorders, such as entrepreneurship and leadership.

In a second version of the model, we see such tendencies as grandiosity, impulsivity, pleasure-seeking, irritation, apathy, and anxiety spread across every possible fear-anger combination—with or without cycling. Version number three incorporates behaviors associated with such conditions as pathological gambling, obsession/ compulsion, and even borderline (though, the authors note, this inclusion is for "didactic purposes" only).

Thus, the $E=MC^2$ of mood becomes the $E=MC^3$ of mood AND personality. Or, taking it a step farther, the $E=MC^4$ of mood AND personality AND environment.

If this suggests a throwback to the ancient Greeks and their black bile and hot winds from Mars and all the rest, you are absolutely correct. Same map, in effect, different imagery. It almost doesn't matter what goes on the map or where we place things so long as we acknowledge the interplay of all the forces inside and around us and how each exerts an effect on the other. If we must include symptom lists, they exist as rough guides only.

Nothing is static, everything is changing. At the same time, though, hidden but pervasive is that strange entity—that mysterious dark energy of the universe—we refer to as "normal." It may not exist on anyone's map, as such, but the mere existence of such a map demands we direct our attention toward it.

So when we find ourselves touching down upon it—this strange place called "normal"—what can we expect? If fear and anger govern our lives, our "normal" is going to look an awful lot like a personality disorder. At the very least, it's going to be consistent with any number of unenviable behavioral traits that leave us stuck in our misery and turn people against us.

"Fear is the path of the Dark Side. Fear leads to anger, anger leads to hate, hate leads to suffering." Is all of psychiatry and psychology nothing more than a remedial attempt to catch up to Master Yoda?

The suffering cuts two ways. The individuals I encountered trying to set up a state DBSA certainly possessed in abundance this unbearable darkness of being. These were not happy people. But what really impressed me was their sheer unbounded enthusiasm in unloading their miserable surplus on others. I finally got smart and cut them out of my life, but not before a thudding sensation in my head told me I was about to sink into a monster depression.

Nevertheless, I owe these people a certain debt of reluctant gratitude. You see, in my campaign to figure out their behavior, I was forced to redirect my analytical focus on myself. Call it the Eye of Socrates—know thyself—brutal, uncompromising, unforgiving.

Freud had it wrong. He thought all our scary stuff lurked out of sight in the id, the sub-basement of our unconscious mind. But the actual reality show is going on upstairs, where numerous unwanted houseguests have turned up in our living room. Welcome to normal.

But we only have to look at the four women I highlighted in this book—Willa, Maggie, Maricela, and Therese—to also realize how uplifting normal can be.

In some of us, it may be equivalent to sharing a fine wine with our cultural folk heroes. My version would involve having Einstein and Louis Armstrong and Eleanor Roosevelt drop by for a beer and buffalo wings. Nikola Tesla and Emily Dickinson, too. On my good days, I almost feel my neurons resonating in harmony, all those traits that reflect the best in our nature.

But then Attila the Hun turns up demanding protection money and the reality show spins into its next phase. So it goes …

So who the hell are we? Were it not for our moods, our map of reality might look something like this:

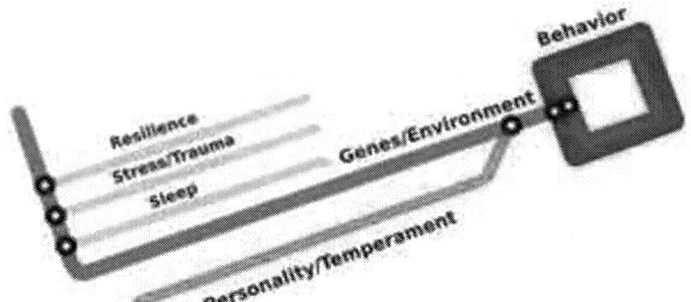

Needless to say, in our case, our moods have a way of hogging the limelight ...

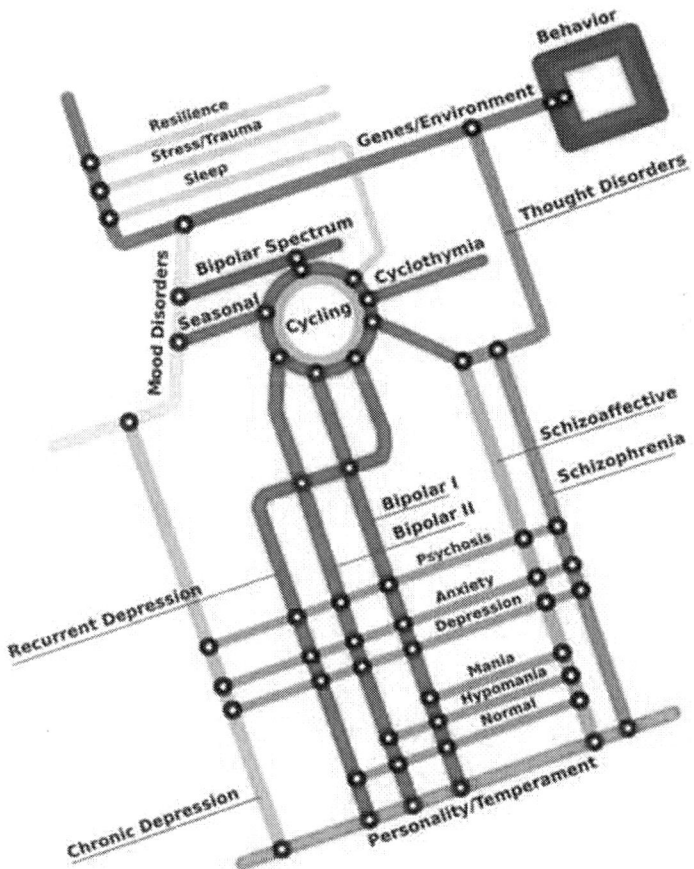

Recall how I introduced you to this map back in Chapter Eleven. If I have done my job, not only will this map start making sense to you, but you will have changed somewhat in how you view bipolar, together with how you see mood and personality interacting. This actually happened to me. Let me explain ...

I had no idea when I began this book of the emphasis I would give to "normal." Once I got several chapters in, though, it became clear I needed to regard normal as a mood episode unto itself, as worthy of our respect as depression and mania and hypomania and anxiety. This was one of those Newton-under-the-apple tree moments for me. From there, "normal" literally took over the book.

Thus, if our "normal" fails us, our depressions and manias and anxieties are sure to follow suit. Or, looking at it from a slightly different perspective, if our normal is too fragile, depression and mania and anxiety are going to come crashing through the door. This is where the Socratic injunction to "know thyself" acquires a new sense of urgency.

Contrast, for a second, how we look at depression and mania. We tend to see them as entities apart from ourselves. We may even give them names, such as "the beast" or the "black dog." I tend to call my depression "Fred," familiar yet apart. This frees me to view my moods with a sense of detachment.

It also confers on me a sense of absolution. I'm sure a lot of you felt this way when you were first diagnosed—it's not you, it's something else, this strange force. Of all things, you may have been engulfed in a wave of blessed relief. I'm really okay—it's all the fault of Fred or the beast or whomever.

"Normal" doesn't let us off the hook so easily. It's personal, it's painful. We have to come to terms with ourselves. In the long run, though, our enquiry is the source of our salvation. In my next book, we will be exploring normal in great depth—our personality and its attendant behaviors.

This includes both the good and the bad, which are inevitably found in the same personality traits. Thus, our tendency toward introversion may cut us off from the world and set us up for our next depression. But it may also open us up to a deep and rich inner world that the extravert majority cannot possibly imagine.

We will also delve deeper into creativity, and extend our enquiry into intuition and nonlinear thinking. People who think nonlinearly, for example, may see problems before they eventuate, as well as their solutions. This is the type of adaptive advantage that got us out of our caves, but is also the source of tremendous misunderstanding, especially if those around us have already written us off as crazy.

Whose reality is it, anyway? Cognitive psychology has advanced the airtight case that we are deluding ourselves if we believe in the powers of rational thinking. It doesn't exist. The brain is simply making stuff up and tricking us into thinking we're thinking. To some of us, this news may come as a tremendous relief.

We will also be taking a look at behaviors acknowledged by all and sundry as undesirable—anger, selfishness, and so on—as well as those regarded as admirable, such as gratitude and altruism. We will also explore the ins and outs of personal character, which includes virtues such as honesty and their polar opposites too numerous to mention.

In addition, we will investigate our sense of being different—the type of behavioral quirks and eccentricities that endear us to people on one hand and cut us off from humanity on the other. To thine own self be true, but at what cost?

Finally, we will be casting a hard uncompromising eye at whether our genes and environment doom us to lead miserable lives, or whether we can dare imagine better ones for ourselves. There exist no shortage of self-help books, but from our vantage point they all fail on one basic level—namely they do not account for how our bipolar manages to simultaneously drag us down and throw us off track every step of the way.

So, just as we folded in personality in this book on moods, so we will fold in mood to my next book on personality and behavior.

The connecting link, of course, is "normal." Where this book ends, the next one begins. Normal, as we have seen, can be an extremely frightening place. But it is also the repository of all that is good inside us, together with all our hopes and dreams.

Normal is the true starting point in our journey to know thyself, as well as the final destination. In normal, we find our sense of home, as well as our sense of coming home. In one sense, our journey never ends. In another, we have already arrived, even if we don't know it yet. Welcome to normal. Welcome home.

32. CALL TO ACTION

This is a good time to remind you once more that this is the first book in *The Bipolar Expert Series*. I am looking to have my next book out in 2016, and I need your help. You are my panel of experts.

Ever since I first began writing about bipolar, I have always regarded my efforts as a collaboration with my readers. Over the years, your wisdom and experience has guided me. You have been the source of my ideas, my mentors, my reality check, and the reason I get up in the morning.

Now, I'm looking to move our relationship to the next level. My next book will be about you. I need to hear from you. I need you to tell me what it's like being you. This will be a two-way conversation: I will be raising my own talking points. But I'm also looking to hear what matters to you.

Ordinarily, this is where I would ask you to follow me on Facebook and Twitter and go to my website and all the rest. But to make this work, you need to be on my mailing list. To this end, I have set up a special page on my new website. All you have to do is click on the link on this page enter your email address in the form.

Again, you are my panel of experts. Please join me.

http://www.bipolarexpertseries.com/expertpanel1.html

And now, to end on a high note, the following bonus chapter …

33. JAMMIN' WITH THE SCIENTISTS

A strange request turned up on my Twitter feed. A certain New York MD—let's call her Jill—wanted to know if anyone in San Diego had a didgeridoo to spare. I live just outside of San Diego. I play the didgeridoo.

It turns out Jill was organizing an evening drum circle for a medical conference at a famous historic resort on Coronado Island. One of the conference-goers needed a didgeridoo. I could do her one better and bring along eight or nine. No, I'm not making this up.

In case you're wondering: None of the many psychiatric conferences I had attended over the years ever featured a drum circle, much less sought out people with didgeridoo experience. But this was no ordinary conference. The people who run it—an organization called Singularity University—are the very people you see giving TED Talks.

Ray Kurzweil, for instance, is an inventor and the author of the 2005 *New York Times* best-seller, *The Singularity is Near*, which imagines a not too distant tomorrow when artificial intelligence overtakes human intelligence. This doesn't mean a dystopian future. But the future will certainly be different. It could be that we will have implants in our brains that give us the ability to access all information on the cloud, and even download what we need. We could also insure our own immortality by uploading our memories.

One of the conferences that Singularity University stages is *Exponential Medicine*. The people who attend are thinkers and doers very happy to pay $4,000 for four days of hanging out with fellow thinkers and doers. The face of medicine is changing. If you are, say, a dental professional involved in making customizable teeth and jaws using 3-D printing technology, this is your chance to shoot the breeze with a therapist exploring the practical applications of real time brainwave downloads into your smartphone.

The keynoter for this year's event is Craig Venter, the scientist enfant terrible famous for sequencing the human genome and creating life in the lab. Once Jill and I connect on the phone, I know my plans are changing for the day. As well as showing up with my didgeridoos, I will be attending as a journalist. My media credentials are waiting.

Didgeridoos in the trunk, quick stop at Guitar Center to pick up a new jack for my portable sound system, off we go …

Late afternoon, Hotel del Coronado, "the Del," featured in the Marilyn Monroe classic, *Some Like it Hot*. Outside, the sun is lighting the Pacific, but we're in a dark room listening to Dr Venter. In response to a question from the audience concerning whether it is possible to create a super-human, Dr Venter replies: "If you can define one, we can create one."

Mind-boggling, but a bit scary. This is a conversation everyone needs to be in on, but is psychiatry even aware of one going on? What was their conversation, I wondered, and who was participating in it? And why would anyone even care?

Same room, a couple of hours later. The drapes have been thrown open. We catch the last of the sun. We set up a mini drum circle. I pass out a couple of didgeridoos and start making noise. I'm jammin' with the scientists.

Next day, as I listen to one cutting-edge speaker after another and engage in conversations with some very bright people, I can't help but question the relevance of psychiatry. The year before—to near-unanimous universal indifference—the APA had published its DSM-5. Now, I wonder ...

Imagine an open-source DSM—what that would look like and who would participate. In an open-source world, no diagnostic bible would be credible without massive input from patients. Neither would any treatment modality.

As if on cue, throughout the day and into the next two, speaker after speaker points out that the pace of change demands that patients assume center stage in the conversation. Putting their money where their mouth is, the conference even devotes one session to a panel of patients. Other sessions show evidence of patient handiwork.

You might say the seeds for this series of books were sown at that conference. Yes, back in 2006 I had broken new ground in writing the kind of book that only doctors were supposed to author. But now I needed to step outside the safety of my profession. Instead of merely reporting as a journalist and sticking in my occasional two cents, I would assert my authority as an expert patient.

But my lived experience makes no sense without the collective wisdom of the highly dedicated scientists and clinicians I featured in this book. Future books will take a similar approach—scientific wisdom through patient eyes, my eyes, your eyes. Scientific discovery and innovation is exploding at an exponential pace, but we the patients represent the essential reality check. Always, always, we need to be talking—and talking back.

Evening, second day of the conference. We're on the beach. Over at one end, table and chairs have been set up for dinner. Hotel staff are applying the finishing touches to the buffet. Bar service is now open. A bonfire is going.

Conference attendees start streaming in from the hotel.

Further over, a group of us are arranging chairs into a giant drum circle. Two expert drummers—one who I recognize from the local drummer community—have brought a supply of djembes—west African drums—and other noise-makers. They will be leading the circle.

There exists a lot of convincing expert evidence on the mental health benefits of drumming, and by extension the didgeridoo. And, for all I know, a lot of that evidence could well have come from the people now enjoying dinner on the beach. Actually, there is one such person— Adam Gazzely, a neuroscientist from UCSF. I missed his talk from the previous morning, but I was present a few months before at a drum circle he addressed.

Yes, a neuroscientist speaking at a drum circle. It's a long story involving a collaboration with Mickey Hart, drummer with the legendary Grateful Dead, but I digress ...

No surprise, Jill the MD is an adept djembe-player. She lives in New York and knows the same didge-player there as I do. Small world.

My portable sound system is hooked up. My didgeridoos are stacked against two chairs. The drummers and I have warmed up. At the last moment, a woman friend of mine materializes to help me out. The doctors and scientists—not to mention a venture capitalist or two —start wandering over from their dinners. The expert drummers start strapping some them into djembes, and give them quick demos.

Some gravitate to my didgeridoos. My friend and I start handing them out and show them how to buzz their lips into a vulgar raspberry noise. Four to six feet of hollow tubing transforms that raspberry into some of the most profound resonances to ever grace the human ear.

But tonight is not about beauty or perfection, or all the amazing things a skilled performer can do with a length of pipe. It's the joy of making noise, connecting with others, being playful, getting out of your rational mind and being a kid again. I don't have to explain. They get it. That's why they're here.

The drummers get a rhythm going. Over in the didgeridoo section, we start blasting away. For the next hour or so, some of the smartest people in the world wander in and out of our circle. We're laughing and joking, making merry. This is southern California. We are on a beach. This is what life is all about.

Later, my friend and I kick off our shoes and we enjoy a quiet walk along the waves. My mind is in harmony, at rest. Off to one side in the distance are lights from the Point Loma headlands. Straight ahead way over the horizon is Asia. Behind us is the Del, all lit up. It's been a perfect day. Sometimes, we just can't help ourselves. Every once in a while, life, against all our expectations, just happens to turn out right.

Thank you for reading this. Until the next book in this series …

END MATTER

ABOUT JOHN MCMANAMY

I am an award-winning mental health writer and author, living in the San Diego area. In 1999, soon after I was diagnosed with bipolar, I began researching and writing about my illness. This led to the 2006 publication of my book, *Living Well with Depression and Bipolar Disorder*. Frederick Goodwin, former head of the NIMH, called it "a vast trove of knowledge and insight." Nassir Ghaemi, now at Tufts, said "it breaks new ground." Susan Bergeson, then president of DBSA, called it "the perfect book for those living with mood disorders."

When not writing about bipolar, I enjoy getting out in nature and playing the didgeridoo.

Where to find me ...

The Bipolar Expert Series (website):
www.bipolarexpertseries.com

The Bipolar Expert Series (blog):
http://blog.bipolarexpertseries.com

The Bipolar Expert Series (Facebook page):
https://www.facebook.com/bipolarexpertseries

@johnmcman (Twitter handle): https://twitter.com/johnmcman

And, once again, I ask you to join me on my panel of experts. Please click the link below to sign up:
http://www.bipolarexpertseries.com/expertpanel1.html

ABOUT THE BIPOLAR EXPERT SERIES

The Bipolar Expert Series is a publishing project founded by John McManamy, author of *Living Well with Depression and Bipolar Disorder*. The project is aimed at helping you become your own expert patient, with six books covering every aspect of bipolar disorder.

These include (titles two through six are tentative) ...

NOT JUST UP AND DOWN, published Nov 2015, on our moods.

NORTH OF NORMAL, scheduled for publication the middle of 2016, on our behavior.

INTO RECOVERY, scheduled for publication late 2016/early 2017, on recovery.

YOUR BRAIN AND HOW TO USE IT, scheduled for publication late 2017, on what makes us tick, or not.

THESE MEDS AREN'T WORKING, scheduled for publication sometime in 2018, on what you need to do to make your treatments and therapies work for you.

I'M PERFECTLY SANE, YOU'RE THE ONE WITH THE PROBLEM, scheduled for publication in either 2018 or 2019), on bipolar relationships.

Again, please join my panel of experts:
http://www.bipolarexpertseries.com/expertpanel1.html

ACKNOWLEDGEMENTS

This book would not have been possible without the support and encouragement of a network of highly valued friends, not to mention some online acquaintances who came out of the woodwork and generously offered to lend a hand. These include:

Louise Woo, a dear longtime friend and my mother confessor, who initially put the idea of a self-publishing a series of bipolar books into my head, and kept encouraging me throughout.

Joanne Shortell, who advocates for the rights of those with service animals (she can help you at servicepoodle.com/contact-us). It was Joanne who got me started on the project. She came up with the titles for both *The Bipolar Expert Series* and NOT JUST UP AND DOWN. In addition, she tipped me off to Scrivener's book-writing software, which spared me tons of time and frustration, plus she gave me some good pointers on marketing my work. As if that weren't enough, she took a cold hard look at my initial draft and came back to me with what amounted to a professional-quality structural edit.

This changed everything about the book, literally everything.

Sally Shepherd, local mental health advocate and personal mentor, who had a look at my draft once I got it into decent shape, and came up with many helpful suggestions.

Tina Wherry and Kathryn Case, two Facebook friends who know what they are doing, who set aside major chunks of their precious time to give my manuscript the eagle eye. The result was a finished product, but more important—two new people in my life.

And, of course: Willa, Maggie, Maricela, and Therese.

I also need to single out two bipolar bloggers I greatly admire, who truly care about the people they write for, and who make me feel I am not alone—Natasha Tracy and Jessica Gimeno. Natasha's *Breaking Bipolar* blog can be found on *HealthyPlace*, plus she hosts her own blog, *Bipolar Burble*. Jessica, who has a wisdom beyond her years, posts her own *Fashionably Ill* blog. A Google search will take you right where you need to be.

Plus Gina Pera, all around fearless advocate and totally hilarious person, who writes on adult ADHD, including her blog *The ADHD Roller Coaster* and her book, *Is It You or Me or Adult ADD*. Gina has a singular way of making me feel like the two of us are the only voices of reason in a world that has totally lost its mind. This is perfectly true, of course.

Two people outside the mental health community who kept me sane throughout this effort include Mara Clear Spring Cook and Jessica Neagle. At just the right moments, they would get me out of the house and into the fresh air, often around the fire to the sound of drums and didgeridoos. Or else they would just plain check in or come up with an excuse to hang out. In short, two fast friends who have my back.

Okay, so far it's been all women. Sometimes, I feel men are totally irrelevant to the future of our species, but I will leave that for another book outside this series. The men here are represented by the researchers I have relied on in this book, whose work has greatly informed my own views of bipolar.

I first came across Frederick Goodwin in 2000 at the DBSA national conference in Boston, though I was too insecure at the time to work up the courage to introduce myself. Just to get to that conference, I had to fight my way through panic attacks that physically mimicked cardiac events. A year later, in better mental shape, I finally got the chance to introduce myself to him at the Fourth International Conference on Bipolar Disorder in Pittsburgh. In 2002, at the DBSA conference in Cleveland, I was singularly impressed to find him sitting at the breakfast table with the ordinary conference-goers rather than the bipolar royalty. That's the kind of man he is.

I first met Nassir Ghaemi at the 2002 APA annual meeting in Philadelphia. I'm sure I asked him a lot of dumb questions, but he was most gracious in his responses, as if he had all the time in the world for me. As an aside—in journalism, it's not the questions you ask, but the answers you get. Dr Ghaemi would also email me with his reactions to my newsletters, as if I carried some weight in the research community. I kept running into him at conferences, and naturally a friendship developed.

I got a chance to become acquainted with Hagop Akiskal once I moved to the San Diego area. What stands out most about Dr Akiskal is his passion and sense of purpose. In pursuit of what he believes is right, he is not afraid to butt heads with the psychiatric establishment— and often does. In short, the kind of man I can relate to. I had the pleasure of sitting with him over a NAMI San Diego award dinner in 2012. He was being honored with a research award. I was the one who nominated him.

Okay, one more man, my brother James. Way back, on the east coast, he was the one who took me to the emergency room when I was in a state of crisis. This set the scene for my coming to terms and eventual recovery. Years later, he followed me out to southern California. At my place, over beers and Neil Young, we would rehash our childhoods. Thus began a new stage in my healing. One day, over beers and Neil Young, we found other things to talk about. That's the way it works.

It wouldn't be right it I didn't pay tribute to my readers and those in the bipolar community—many who have followed and encouraged me since Day One. Perhaps you are one of them. But even if you came across me only today, you are a valued part of my tribe. For nearly two decades, you have not only given me a reason to wake up in the morning, but given me something to look forward to.

By necessity, this book focused on scientific research. But my perceptions have been equally shaped, if not more so, by people like you—patients and loved ones. A lot of what you read in this book had its origins from reader comments to my pieces, from email queries, from discussions at support group meetings, and talking to people everywhere, whether at mental health conferences or around a campfire or jammed into the seat of a plane. Often, I yearn for a life away from bipolar—where I'm making a living writing novels or rolling dough in a pizzeria—and not having to identify as someone living with a mental illness. But you guys have a way of pulling me back in.

Finally, a tip of my hat to some of those who have proved major influences in my bipolar life over the years:

Colleen Sullivan, founder of the website *Bipolar World*, who first urged me to start writing about my illness, held my hand in those initial stages, and thus set my life on a new course.

Kathy Flaherty who was present at the very first support group I walked into back in 1999 in Connecticut. She has dedicated her life to championing the afflicted and powerless, and we've remained good friends ever since.

Sue Bergeson, an early fan of my email newsletter and confidence-booster and wonderful human being, who later joined DBSA and became its head. She later moved into the private sector, where she is breaking down barriers from the inside.

Janice Papolos, co-author of *The Bipolar Child* and one of my biggest cheerleaders and totally delightful person, who got my *Living Well with Bipolar Disorder* manuscript in front of the one editor who knew what to do with it.

Bill Allman, who recruited me to write for the website, *HealthCentral*, that actually paid me, and thus brought a measure of financial security into my life. Bill was a pioneer champion of the expert patient and treated his contributors as his star reporters.

Tom Wootton, author of the *The Bipolar Advantage*, who coached me in public speaking, which removed a lot of the fear in my getting up before an audience. The most profound effect, though, had to do with me being able to relax around people in smaller settings, thus freeing me to start enjoying my life.

Paul Cumming, all-purpose advocate, who encouraged me to come out to the San Diego area after my world fell apart on the east coast. The move set the scene for a new and unexpected chapter in my recovery and healing.

Rick Heller, San Diego coffee buddy and intellectual sparring partner.

This brings me to Kevin Greim, to whom this book is dedicated. He walked into our Princeton NJ support group, a kid with a baseball cap on backward, goofy look on his face. We heard his story. It was the story of a sincere young man in a state of upheaval with nowhere to turn. The people in our group had a way of making him feel he had come to the right place. A rapport developed. He came back the next week. Then became a regular.

Kevin possessed a wisdom well beyond his years. In no time, he emerged as one of the group's leaders. Even people twice and three times his age sought out his wise counsel. At the same time, he was a bringer of joy. A fast friendship soon developed. Then my life turned upside down. There was a tearful farewell, then I was in California. One evening two years later, I arrived home to a chilling message on my answering machine: the morning before, he had taken his life. He was 28.

Life has no answers. But that doesn't stop us from searching for meaning. Who knows why we were put on earth, but if anyone asks I will say it's because of Kevin, my good friend. Nothing more to say …

RESOURCES

I'm going to limit this to a few key groups and information sites that I can vouch for ...

Mental Health Advocacy, Education, and Support Organizations

These groups are national in scope, with numerous local and state affiliates. On a local level, these organizations offer an array of support services, plus its members can be indispensable in connecting you or your loved one with other groups, not to mention social and medical and therapeutic services. You can get local contact info, plus educational information, by going to the national sites. These include:

National Alliance on Mental Illness (NAMI):
https://www.nami.org

Mental Health America (MHA):
http://www.mentalhealthamerica.net

Depression and Bipolar Support Alliance (DBSA):
http://www.dbsalliance.org

Mood Disorders Association of Canada:
http://www.mooddisorderscanada.ca

Educational Resources

International Bipolar Foundation (IBPF): http://

ibpf.org

CREST.BD: http://www.crestbd.ca

McMan's Depression and Bipolar Web: http://www.mcmanweb.com

In the UK

I can't personally vouch for patient advocacy organizations in the UK. Here are two that appear to be useful points of first contact:

BipolarUK:
http://www.bipolaruk.org.uk

Mind:
http://www.mind.org.uk

NOTES

This space is for sources that didn't receive adequate recognition in the main text, and for various sundry asides.

Chapter One
Getting to know us

An editorial in the March 27, 2004 *British Medical Journal* mentioned two Stanford University studies that found that so-called expert patients with chronic diseases felt better and had 40 percent fewer doctor visits than the other patients in the studies.

Chapter Two
An introduction to cycles

Depending on the source, Falret came up with circular insanity in either 1851 or 1854. The best way to explain the discrepancy is that he informally published in 1851, then formally in 1854.

All direct references to Kraepelin are from the English translation to his celebrated 1921 *Manic-Depressive Insanity*. Without question, after nearly one century, this fairly short work remains the best book ever written on bipolar. His *Manic-Depressive Insanity* was part of a four-volume magnum opus, *Compendium der Psychiatrie*, which he first published in 1883. In all he published nine versions of *Compendium*. The last, which appeared in 1927, a year after his death, was ten times the length of his first.

Kraepelin's output reveals his evolving views on manic-depression over the years. Thus, in this book, you will find references to the 1899 and 1915 versions of the master. For these insights, I am reliant on the scholarship of Goodwin and Jamison in their 2007 *Manic Depressive Illness: Bipolar Disorders and Recurrent Depression*, Oxford University Press, (Goodwin and Jamison in future citations) and other sources.

Goodwin and Jamison has the heft of a Gutenberg Bible, and is just as valuable.

Another key source was the 2000 book, *Bipolar Disorders: 100 Years After Manic-Depressive Insanity*, Springer, (Marneros and Angst, for future reference) a focused collection of essays from numerous luminaries, edited by Andreas Marneros and Jules Angst. Their introduction provides an excellent Kraepelin appreciation.

In the interests of narrative simplicity, I focus on Kraepelin at the expense of his predecessors and contemporaries, most notably Wilhelm Weygandt.

Chapter Four
Evolution of the Standard Version

Most of this chapter is based on my own textual analysis of Kraepelin and the DSMs I and II.

The Rosenhan Experiment citation: David Rosenhan, "On Being Sane in Insane Places," Jan 1973 *Science*.

Chapter Five

The DSM: How the most influential psychiatrist ...

There exists no shortage of accounts on the making of the DSM-III. My principal sources included:

- Hannah Decker, "How Kraepelinian was Kraepelin? How Kraepelinian are the neo-Kraepelinians?—from Emil Kraepelin to DSM-III," published in *History of Psychiatry*, Sage Publications, 2007.
- Kenneth Kendler et al, "The Development of the Feighner Criteria: A Historical Perspective," in the Feb 2010 *American Journal of Psychiatry*.
- Kirk and Hutchins, *The Selling of the DSM, The Rhetoric of Science in Psychiatry*, Aldine de Gruyter, 1992

Back in the fifties and sixties, George Winokur was one of the few American psychiatrists making a serious scientific investigation of manic-depression. His 1969 book, *Manic Depressive Illness*, is perhaps most noteworthy for the fact that it is heavily reliant on his own studies.

Chapter Six
The DSM: Busting the myth

See Kirk and Hutchins, op cit.

Until taking over as head of the DSM-5, Dr Kupfer was head of the Department of Psychiatry at the University of Pittsburgh. The university and its affiliate, the Western Psychiatric Institute and Clinic, is noted worldwide for its research and treatment of mood disorders. Dr Kupfer has made outstanding contributions to the field of bipolar research.

The people comprising the DSM-5's mood disorders workgroup represented the best minds in the field, but the problems they faced were manifold, including the obvious fact that real change does not come from inside the established order. Others included:

- Setting the evidence bar for new diagnostic criteria way too high. This, ironically, meant that the workgroup kept in a lot of old and suspect stuff that had never been subjected to adequate scientific scrutiny in the first place.
- Also, advances in brain science appeared to make the workgroup members doubt their own judgment. It was as if no one wanted to look foolish coming up with new stuff.
- Finally, as Nassir Ghaemi pointed in a May 5, 2013 blog on *Psychology Today*, the DSM-5 committees comprised in large part those who had worked on previous DSMs. These people were in their thirty-and-forty-somethings then. Now they were in their sixties and seventies. The next generation was frozen out.

Regarding depression in men, I urge you to read Terrence Real's *I Don't Want to Talk About It: Overcoming the Secret Legacy of Male Depression,* Scribner, 1998

Chapter Seven
The DSM: Killing Buddha

Regarding antipsychiatry, once we grasp the fact that

psychiatry essentially lied to us concerning the DSM, we can easily see where these individuals are coming from. To a person, these people see themselves as "survivors" of a system that has mistreated, abused, and ultimately failed them.

They are not alone. General distrust is rampant. Psychiatry is going through its worst credibility problem since the 1970s.

Thomas Szasz's 1962 book, *The Myth of Mental Illness,* was highly influential in its day, but fell out of favor once scientific discoveries began demonstrating how our biology (which includes how we react to our environment) influences our behavior. Despite all evidence to the contrary, Dr Szasz clung to his views till his death in 2012.

Two milestone discoveries I came across in San Francisco in 2003 included a 2002 brain scan study by Hariri and Weinberger that showed a plausible connection between a gene variation and an emotion, while a 2003 population study by Caspi and Moffit showed a strong link between that same gene variation and stress-induced depression.

These studies and others proved major game-changers in our understanding of human behavior. The citations:

- Hariri et al, "Serotonin transporter genetic variation and the response of the human amygdala," July 2002 *Science.*
- Caspi et al, "Influence of life stress on depression: moderation by a polymorphism in the 5-HTT gene," July 2003 *Science.*

The source for the 1,200 patients-a-month figure: Gardner Harris, "Talk Doesn't Pay, So Psychiatry Turns Instead to Drug Therapy," March 5, 2011 *New York Times*. The article is based on a lengthy interview with a Pennsylvania psychiatrist, Donald Levin, who voiced his frustrations in shooing patients out the door after ten or 15 minutes in order to meet the demands of a health care system that makes no sense.

The Dr Koukopoulos anecdote comes from an obituary in the Oct 2013 *Journal of Bipolar Disorders*.

Chapter Eight
Personality and Temperament

An enlightening commentary on personality and temperament traits in bipolar, one that gives Galen the Physician his due, can be found in a chapter by Jules Angst in Marneros and Angst.

For more insight into Shakespeare and temperament, check out Sarah Holland's 1998 student thesis, *Hamlet: A Humoral Diagnosis*, which you can find online.

Some commentators discuss the four humors in the context of pre-modern thinkers naively attributing our moods to mysterious bodily fluids. This is wrong and totally misses the point. In the absence of scientific instruments, the ancients cultivated a keen sense of observation and insight that is often sorely lacking in modern medicine.

Chapter Nine

Is it normal or is it bipolar?

Leonard Bernstein was a major champion of Mahler. A 1981 article, "Mahler: His Time Has Come," can be found on *Leonardbernstein.com*. See also his Fifth Norton Lecture from 1973, posted on *YouTube*.

Chapter Ten
Bipolar—here we are …

The Amish study citation: Janice Egeland et al, "Prospective study of prodromal features for bipolarity in well Amish children," July 2003 *Journal of the American Academy of Child Adolescent Psychiatry*.

I could not find this study in Goodwin and Jamison, nor a discussion of prodromal symptoms in the context of brain development. Goodwin and Jamison, however, referenced a much earlier Egeland study in which she originally identified her Amish adult bipolar population. The cultural context posed new challenges for the researchers. This passage from Goodwin and Jamison is too good to leave out:

For example, manic behaviors to the Amish include racing one's horse and carriage too fast, buying or using machinery or worldly items, using the public telephone excessively, and planning vacations during the wrong season.

The usual progression from prodromal features in kids to fully symptomatic episodes in adults hardly rules out instances of advanced bipolar in even very young children. Papolos and Papolos' *The Bipolar Child* (Broadway, 1999) proved a timely wake-up call in this regard. Early childhood is when the brain is extremely active in proceeding from one stage of development to the next. In this light, it is easy to imagine the million things that can go wrong.

Early-onset bipolar remains a controversial topic, but the ignorance and dogma from naysayers hardly sheds light on the issue. There is much we need to learn, but learning is a non-starter without listening.

One example of Beatriz Luna's published work: "In vivo evidence of neurophysiological maturation of the human adolescent striatum," April 2015 *Developmental Cognitive Neuroscience.*

As to bipolar experts not talking to schizophrenia experts and vice-versa, it's not just me. This was the topic of a talk Carol Tamminga gave to a session at the 2007 International Conference on Bipolar Disorder in Pittsburgh. Dr Tamminga is a leading expert in schizophrenia research at the University of Texas, Dallas. She was also one of the organizers of the 2009 Schizophrenia Congress I attended.

Since bipolar research is an extremely small and narrow field compared to schizophrenia research, it is far more incumbent for bipolar researchers to see what their counterparts in schizophrenia are up to than vice-versa.

To drive this point home, two years later, during Q and A at a session at the 2011 Bipolar Conference, I asked a question that referenced something significant I picked up at the Schizophrenia Congress, and highly germane to the discussion. The panel, all bipolar experts, had no clue what I was talking about.

The Carrie Bearden talk citation: "Risk and Vulnerability for Mood Disorders in Teens Discovery to Recovery: A Path to Healthy Minds," April 30, 2013 *Brain and Behavior Research Foundation.*

The Anne Duffy study citation: "The developmental trajectory of bipolar disorder," Feb 2014 *British Journal of Psychiatry.*

Chapter Eleven
The Map to Reality

I conceived the subway-style map, myself. But without the open-source vector graphics editor, Inkscape, the map never would have left my head. This is professional-quality software—for free. Thank you, Bryce Harrington, founder of Inkscape.

Chapter Twelve
The bipolar spectrum and recurrence

A clear and concise explanation of cycling and the bipolar spectrum is provided by Jim Phelps in his 2006 book, *Why Am I Still Depressed?* McGraw-Hill. Dr Phelps' book, incidentally, is one of the few I can unreservedly recommend written by a psychiatrist for depression and bipolar patients.

Dr Akiskal has written prolifically on the bipolar spectrum. A concise version of his position, with ample footnotes, can be found in his May 21, 2004 *Primary Psychiatry* article, "The Bipolar Spectrum in Psychiatric and General Medical Practice." A longer version can be found in a chapter in Marneros and Angst.

Nassir Ghaemi's view of the spectrum, with Dr Goodwin as a co-author, is spelled in the March, 2002 *Canadian Journal of Psychiatry* article, "'Cade's disease' and beyond: misdiagnosis, antidepressant use, and a proposed definition for bipolar spectrum disorder."

Dr Angst's study supporting a minimum two-day time duration in hypomania: "The evolving epidemiology of bipolar disorder," Oct 2002 *World Psychiatry*.

And his later study supporting a four-day duration: "Prevalence and characteristics of undiagnosed bipolar disorders in patients with a major depressive episode: the BRIDGE study," Aug 2011 *Archives of General Psychiatry*.

A good overview of recurrence in depression appears in the Dec 2007 *Clinical Psychology Review*, "Risk for Recurrence in Depression," by Stephanie Burcusa and William Iacono.

Chapter Thirteen
Connecting "up" and "down"

Dr Koukopoulos does a masterful job explaining cyclicity, including its historical roots, in a chapter in Marneros and Angst.

Further support of our meds interfering with homeostasis is provided in Peter Sterling's article, "Homeostasis vs Allostasis: Implications for Brain Function and Mental Disorders," in the Oct 2014 *JAMA*

Psychiatry.

The Jim Phelps chapter citation: "The Mood Spectrum," *Bipolar II Disorder: Modelling, Measuring and Managing*, (Second Edition) Gordon Parker, editor, April, Cambridge University Press, 2012.

The didgeridoo is an ancient Australian first people wind instrument capable of producing a wide range of unique resonances. The "yidaki," an instrument made by the Yolngu of northeast Arnhem Land, derives from termite-hollowed eucalyptus. The Yolngu have developed a highly virtuosic style of play that can best be described as vocal drumming.

The didgeridoo started to catch on in the West in the 80s and 90s, typically in a droning style of play that suited New Age tastes. Westerners were also quick to tune into the complex harmonics of the didgeridoo and incorporate them into meditative and spiritual healing practices, in much the same manner as drumming and singing bowls.

As the didgeridoo caught on, western musicians began developing their own new styles and techniques, as well as experimenting with new ways of crafting the instrument. The innovations are coming thick and fast. As one player described it, the didgeridoo now is where the electric guitar was in the 50s and 60s.

Chapter Fourteen
The bipolar spectrum and mixed states

A lot of the credit for mixed states goes to Kraepelin's associate, Wilhelm Weygandt, who published on the topic in 1893.

Goodwin and Jamison provide an extensive list of the mixed state prevalence studies.

An example of Dr Koukopoulos writing about mixed states can be found in this article, "Agitated depression as a mixed state and the problem of melancholia," he published in the Sept 1999 *Psychiatric Clinics*.

Much of Dr Akiskal's work on mixed states can be found in *The Journal of Affective Disorders*, where (as of 2011, according to the blog *The Neurocritic*) he has published 165 articles.

One example of Dr Akiskal's state-trait dynamic in action involves an 11-year study on unipolar patients, many who, over time, converted to bipolar. The ones who converted to bipolar were more likely to report mood lability, energy-activity, and daydreaming. The citation: Akiskal et al, "Switching from 'unipolar' to bipolar II. An 11-year prospective study of clinical and temperamental predictors in 559 patients," Feb 1995 *Archives of General Psychiatry*.

A representative mixed state article from Ellen Frank (with Giovanni Cassano and others) includes "The mood spectrum in unipolar and bipolar disorder: arguments for a unitary approach," published in the July 2004 *American Journal of Psychiatry*.

And from Trisha Suppes: "Mixed hypomania in 908 patients with bipolar disorder evaluated prospectively in the Stanley Foundation Bipolar Treatment Network: a sex-specific phenomenon," Oct 2005 *Archives of General Psychiatry*.

The three panelists at the 2015 Psychiatric and Mental Health Congress session comprised Michael Thase of the University of Pennsylvania, Joseph Calabrese of Case Western Reserve, and Gary Sachs of Harvard.

Chapter Fifteen
Kindling and neuroplasticity

Goodwin and Jamison provide an extensive review of post-Kraepelin studies that support kindling.

A study on the aging that Colin Depp was involved in: Dilip Jeste et al, "Older Age is Associated with More Successful Aging: Role of Resilience and Depression," Feb 2013 *American Journal of Psychiatry*.

An informative review article by Dr Merzenich: "Brain plasticity-based therapeutics," June 27, 2014 *Frontiers in Human Neuroscience*.

One of the neuroplasticity-meditation studies Sarah Lazar was involved in: "Mindfulness practice leads to increases in regional brain gray matter density," Jan 2011, *Psychiatry Research: Neuroimaging*.

Chapter Seventeen

The Dunner-Gershon-Goodwin article citation: "Heritable factors in the severity of affective illness," Feb 1976 *Biological Psychiatry*.

This misdiagnosis study citation: Frye et al, "Use of health care services among persons who screen positive for bipolar disorder," Dec 2005 *Psychiatric Services*.

The time to a correct diagnosis study citation: Ghaemi et al, "Is bipolar disorder still underdiagnosed? Are antidepressants overutilized?" Jan 1999 *Journal of Affective Disorders*.

The two DBSA studies (note—Until 2002, DBSA was called DMDA):

- Lish et al, "The National Depressive and Manic-depressive Association (DMDA) survey of bipolar members," Aug 1994 *Journal of Affective Disorders*.
- Hirschfeld et al, "Perceptions and impact of bipolar disorder: how far have we really come? Results of the national depressive and manic-depressive association 2000 survey of individuals with bipolar disorder." Feb 2003 *Journal of Clinical Psychiatry*.

Bipolar suicide statistics vary widely. The figures I cite are based on Goodwin and Jamison's review of the studies.

Regarding the proposition that antidepressants and bipolar do not mix:

The American Psychiatric Association, in its 2010 *Practice Guideline for the Treatment of Patients with Major Depressive Disorder*, advises that doctors first rule out the possibility of bipolar before treating patients for depression.

In its 2001 *Practice Guideline for the Treatment of Patients with Bipolar Disorder*, the APA warns against antidepressant as monotherapy, and advises its use only in conjunction with a mood-stabilizing or antipsychotic medication.

A 2011 meta-analysis of ten studies involving more than 3,000 unipolar and bipolar patients found little difference in response between the two groups to an antidepressant but a much higher risk of inducing mania. The citation: Vasquez et al, "Comparison of antidepressant responses in patients with bipolar vs. unipolar depression: a meta-analytic review," Jan 2011 *Pharmacopsychiatry*.

For a commentary on antidepressants and other drugs in treating bipolar, check out Nassir Ghaemi's piece on the Tufts Medical Center website, "Treatment Concepts." In particular, Dr Ghaemi advises: "In sum, antidepressants can act as mood destabilizers, counteracting the benefits of mood stabilizers."

The Akiskal rule of three citation: "Searching for behavioral indicators of bipolar II in patients presenting with major depressive episodes: the 'red sign,' the 'rule of three' and other biographic signs of temperamental extravagance, activation and hypomania." Feb 2005 *Journal of Affective Disorders*.

Re Dr Goodwin and a family member: I have heard this from him in numerous presentations he has given, both to patients' groups and to fellow psychiatrists.

The WHO study citation: Kathleen Merikangas, "Prevalence and Correlates of Bipolar Spectrum Disorder in the World Mental Health Survey Initiative," March 2011 *Archives of General Psychiatry*.

Chapter Eighteen
Is "up" your true normal?

Marilyn Monroe's own physician diagnosed her with manic-depression. Her erratic behavior and tragic early death due to a drug overdose—together with her family history—emphatically supports a bipolar diagnosis. But her larger-than-life personality can hardly be attributed to bipolar alone.

In this chapter, I made a reference to bipolar support groups, which I will discuss in full in a future book. A support group may or may not be for you, but I strongly urge you attend at least three meetings. There is enormous benefit in face-to-face conversations with those who have walked in your shoes.

In Connecticut, for three years I attended a group run by Mental Health America (MHA), a patient advocacy organization. In New Jersey, I was the founding facilitator of a group affiliated with DBSA (Depression and Bipolar Support Alliance, another patient advocacy organization). I facilitated there for three years. These days, I maintain my own personal support network via my friends.

In the interest of keeping the narrative flow going, I chopped out an account of the founding father, Alexander Hamilton, based on John Gartner's portrayal in *The Hypomanic Edge*. In Hamilton, we have a classic study of genius and brilliance undermined by unfortunate risk-taking (he died in a duel). But no ordinary mind could have come up with the legal and financial framework to both found a new nation and to insure its future prosperity.

This poses an interesting thought experiment: If you were a psychiatrist and a young Hamilton came into your office, knowing what you know now, would you prescribe a bipolar med? Would you—in effect—save his life at the risk of destroying your country? Or could you have it both ways? Slow him down a bit so he lived on to become a great President.

The Jan Scott adherence study citation: Pope and Scott, "Do clinicians understand why individuals stop taking lithium?" May 2003 *Journal of Affective Disorders*.

Chapter Nineteen
When "up" goes wrong, part I ...

For the Dr Suppes citation, check out the notes to Chapter Twelve.

For a discussion of anxious temperament: Akiskal et al, "The role of anxious and hyperthymic temperaments in mental disorders: a national epidemiologic study," June 2010 *World Psychiatry*.

For data involving co-occurring anxiety in bipolar: Merikangas et al, "Lifetime and 12-month prevalence of bipolar spectrum disorder in the National Comorbidity Survey replication," May 2007 *Archives of General Psychiatry*.

For three articles relating to how anxiety and panic complicate the course of treatment of bipolar, all involving

Ellen Frank of the University of Pittsburgh:

- "Anxiety as a correlate of response to the acute treatment of bipolar I disorder," June 2000 *American Journal of Psychiatry*.
- "Clinical significance of lifetime panic spectrum symptoms in the treatment of patients with bipolar I disorder," Oct 2002 *Archives of General Psychiatry*.
- "Mood and anxiety spectrum as a means to identify clinically relevant subtypes of bipolar I disorder," Aug 2007 *Bipolar Disorders*.

Chapter Twenty
When "up" goes wrong, part II

In mania especially, showing rather than telling is mandatory. Hence the reason for including Maggie's story. Significantly, Kraepelin's *Manic-Depressive Insanity* was rich in detailed real people observations, complete with photos. Goodwin and Jamison include several pages of subjective first-person accounts, as did my *Living Well* book.

If we have to mention symptoms, Goodwin and Jamison report that in their review of studies, grandiosity and flight of ideas (racing thoughts) occurred in three-quarters of manic patients. It was also common for manic patients to experience depressive symptoms.

Chapter Twenty-One
When "up" goes wrong, part III ...

Goodwin and Jamison offer an excellent rundown on

the manifold uncertainties of the schizoaffective diagnosis.

Concerning overdiagnosis of schizophrenia in African-Americans, here is an article by Caroline Helwick on a medical website: "Schizophrenia May Be Overdiagnosed in Black Patients," July 31, 2012 *Medscape*.

In 2008, a working group of the International Society of Bipolar Disorders proposed eliminating the schizoaffective diagnosis in its entirely. In its place, they would add certain specifiers to bipolar, depression, and schizophrenia. The citation: Malhi et al, "Schizoaffective disorder: diagnostic issues and future recommendations," Feb 2008 *Bipolar Disorders*.

Chapter Twenty-Three
Depression: What is it?

Robert Post's study tracked 258 patients in the Stanley Foundation Network over a year. Three-quarters had bipolar I. As well as experiencing way more depression than mania and hypomania, two-thirds were substantially impacted by their illness, despite being on meds. The citation: Post et al, "Morbidity in 258 bipolar outpatients followed for 1 year with daily prospective ratings on the NIMH life chart method," June 2003 *Journal of Clinical Psychiatry*.

The Gordon Parker 2004 article citation: "Evaluating treatments for the mood disorders: time for the evidence to get real," June 2004 *Australian and New Zealand Journal of Psychiatry*.

And the 2007 citation: "Is depression overdiagnosed?

Yes," Aug 18, 2007 *British Medical Journal.*

The Nassir Ghaemi editorial citation: Ghaemi et al, "Antidepressants from a public health perspective: re-examining effectiveness, suicide, and carcinogenicity," Jan 2013 *Acta Psychiatrica Scandanavica.*

Chapter Twenty-Four
Depression: It's complicated, just ask Lincoln

Doris Kearns Goodwin in her 2006 book, *Team of Rivals,* takes a different approach to Joshua Wolf Shenk. While she acknowledges that Lincoln certainly had a melancholic disposition, she argues that he functioned at far too high a level to have suffered from constant depression throughout his life. This is set out in an Aug 2006 review by James Neuchterlein on *First Things.*

Chapter Twenty-Five
Depressed or thinking deep?

In case you're wondering, it was no accident that I featured four woman in this book. Before we get into that, first, Willa, Maggie, Maricela, and Therese met my criteria as patients who have gone public with their illness and have written about it from a personal perspective. Second, they are people I connected with years ago and regard as good friends. Third, I believe they are people with whom we can all identify.

As to why all women, it's all about numbers. In my experience, women are far more inclined than men to research their illness and do something about it. Women comprise by far most of my readers. I am also inclined to believe that women are far more thoughtful and reflective and open than men. This certainly shows up in comments to my online pieces.

Contrast this with my Mahler-TR-LBJ-Lincoln celebrity line-up. Making history overwhelmingly favored men. In an early draft, I did include Marilyn Monroe, but the addition came across as forced and out-of-place.

For a Darwinian perspective of depression, check out: Edward Hagen, "Evolutionary Theories of Depression: A Critical Review," Dec 2011 *Canadian Journal of Psychiatry.*

Regarding trade-offs, Darwin was obsessed with the thought of peacocks and their showy tails. The tails clearly made the birds easy targets for predators, which seemed to fly in the face of his then-evolving theory of natural selection. Then Darwin figured out that those with the showiest tales also had the best opportunity to mate and pass on their genes. Hence, the trade-off.

Evolutionary psychology is speculative, but it encourages us to look at common psychiatric conditions from outside the traditional disease mindset. This, in turn, yields new insights into human nature.

Regarding depressive realism, a good discussion can be found in Nassir Ghaemi's 2011 book, *A First-Rate Madness.*

Chapter Twenty-Six
Breaking down depression: Agitated vs vegetative ...

For citations on the dangers of treating bipolar with

antidepressants, please check out the notes under Chapter Seventeen.

For a discussion of the problematic nature of atypical depression, see: Gordon Parker et al, "Atypical depression: a reappraisal," Sept 2002 *American Journal of Psychiatry*.

For an historical view of how older generation antidepressants figured in the development of the atypical diagnosis, see: Michael Thase, "New Directions in the Treatment of Atypical Depression," *Journal of Clinical Psychiatry*, 2007, Supplement 3.

For a discussion of why serotonin antidepressants threw researchers and clinicians off the dopamine scent, see: Dunlop and Nemeroff, "The role of dopamine in the pathophysiology of depression," March 2007 *Archives of General Psychiatry*.

Robert Sapolsky of Stanford is the author of a highly informative article, "Taming Stress," in the Sept 2003 *Scientific American*. In the article, he relates how anxiety interacts with depression via the stress pathways. According to Dr Sapolsky, "If anxiety is a crackling, menacing brushfire, depression is a suffocating heavy blanket thrown on top of it."

Chapter Twenty-Seven
Breaking down bipolar depression

For citations on the dangers of treating bipolar with antidepressants, please check out the notes under Chapter Seventeen.

Psychiatry has been appallingly slow in recognizing that men and women face different environmental risks and social expectations, have different life experiences, have subtly different brain structures, experience notably different hormonal flows, and, not surprisingly, often respond in behaviorally different manners than men.

Chapter Twenty-Nine
Is crazy your true normal? Creativity, genius, and leadership

One of Dr Andreasen's writings on the creativity-bipolar connection includes: "The relationship between creativity and mood disorders," June 2008, *Dialogues in Clinical Neuroscience*.

In a March 2009 blog post on *Psychology Today*, Scott Barry Kaufman outlines how low latent inhibition may apply to both schizophrenia and creativity. For a scholarly review by the same author, see: Kaufman and Paul, "Creativity and schizophrenia spectrum disorders across the arts and sciences," Nov 2014 *Frontiers in Psychology*.

Two key brain scan studies involving difficulties in executive function in the bipolar population:

- Gruber et al, "Decreased activation of the anterior cingulate in bipolar patients: an fMRI study," Oct 2004 *Journal of Affective Disorders*.
- Strakowski et al, "Abnormal FMRI brain activation in euthymic bipolar disorder patients during a counting Stroop interference task," Sept 2005 *American Journal of Psychiatry*.

The Swedish study citation: Simon Kyaga et al, "Creativity and mental disorder: family study of 300,000 people with severe mental disorder," Nov 2011 British Journal of Psychiatry.

Chapter Thirty

The Ghaemi borderline personality disorder citation: "Bipolar Spectrum: A Review of the Concept and a Vision for the Future," Sept 2013 *Psychiatry Investigation*.

The Akiskal borderline citation: Akiskal et al, "Borderline: an adjective in search of a noun," Feb 1985 *Journal of Clinical Psychiatry*.

A couple more examples from the bad old days: Right into the 70s, schizophrenia was believed to be the result of bad parenting, usually in the form of an overbearing mother and a weak father. These horrible moms were labeled as "schizophrenogenic." The thinking also bled over into bipolar, which was often confused with schizophrenia.

Theodore Lidz, the man who dreamed up the schizophrenogenic label, was a professor in psychiatry at Yale. That's how bad it was. Even into the 90s, Dr Lidz was arguing that biological psychiatry was "barking up the wrong tree."

Katie Cadigan's excellent 2009 documentary, *When Medicine Got It Wrong*, frames NAMI's founders—parents who had been labeled as "schizophrenogenic" by psychiatry—as heroes who fought back against the establishment, and who, in the process, changed attitudes.

One more example: At a 2011 NAMI CA convention in Sacramento, Cameron Carter of UC Davis told a story of how as a student in the UK back in the late 70s, he came across a library journal article, hot off the press, that contained the first brain scan evidence of a biological link to schizophrenia. "Bollocks!" someone had scribbled on the page.

The outspoken Fuller Torrey—researcher and advocate—devotes a whole book to how the legacy of Freud held back for decades the advancement of psychiatric research and treatment: *Freudian Fraud: The Malignant Effect of Freud's Theory on American Thought and Culture*, Lucas Books, 1999.

The May 2009 *American Journal of Psychiatry* devotes much of its issue to borderline personality disorder. A number of articles trace the evolution of the diagnosis, from clinical observations of patients who failed to fit the standard Freudian mold, but who nevertheless deemed their behavior the result of bad parenting. As Freud and psychoanalysis became discredited, a newer generation of psychiatrists were inclined to view borderline as a variant of depression or bipolar rather than as an illness in its own right. Only fairly recently, in the wake of fairly convincing research support, has the diagnosis come into its own.

Articles in the issue include:

- Kernberg and Michels, "Editorial: Borderline Personality Disorder."
- John Oldham, "Borderline Personality Disorder Comes of Age."

- Glen Gabbard, "Insight, Transference Interpretation, and Therapeutic Change in the Dynamic Psychotherapy of Borderline Personality Disorder."
- Marianne Goodman et al, "Quieting the Affective Storm of Borderline Personality Disorder."
- John Gunderson, "Borderline Personality Disorder: Ontogeny of a Diagnosis."

The Minzenberg citation: Minzenberg et al, "A neurocognitive model of borderline personality disorder: effects of childhood sexual abuse and relationship to adult social attachment disturbance," Winter 2008 *Development and Psychopathology*.

Various versions of Marsha Linehan's "third-degree burn" quote have been widely disseminated, including in *Time* magazine. Her first published use appears to be in her 1993 book, *Cognitive-Behavioral Treatment of Borderline Personality Disorder*, Guilford Press.

Barbara Oakley's 2008 book, *Evil Genes: Why Rome Fell, Hitler Rose, Enron Failed, and My Sister Stole My Mother's Boyfriend*, looks at personality disorders in the context of the "successfully sinister" who get away with making everyone's life miserable, and often prospering in the process. The profile indicates a combination of traits across different diagnoses, thus blurring categorical distinctions. Thus, the "borderpath," which also includes a generous helping of narcissism.

FINALLY ...

If you actually read through my notes, then I know—totally know—that you are a dedicated follower. Let's stay in touch. First, more books are in the pipeline, not to mention articles and blog posts. This means I can use your help in shaping my ideas and in getting the word out.

Once again, where to find me ...

The Bipolar Expert Series (website):
www.bipolarexpertseries.com

The Bipolar Expert Series (blog):
http://blog.bipolarexpertseries.com

The Bipolar Expert Series (Facebook page):
https://www.facebook.com/bipolarexpertseries

@johnmcman (Twitter handle):
https://twitter.com/johnmcman

But most important, I need you to join my panel of experts. My next book is all about you, and you are the true expert. We need to have a two-way conversation. These conversations will shape my next book. Together, we can make a difference. Here's the link to my sign-up page. Talk soon ...
   http://www.bipolarexpertseries.com/expertpanel1.html

INDEX

Made in the USA
Middletown, DE
07 August 2019